KEYING:

THE POWER OF POSITIVE FEELINGS

USE POWERFUL FEELINGS TO GET ANYTHING YOU WANT!

Donald E. Dossey, Ph.D.

Outcomes Unlimited Press, Inc.

Los Angeles, CA, U.S.A

Fifth printing

Outcomes Unlimited Press, Inc.
Publisher
1015 Gayley Avenue, Ste.1165
Los Angeles, California 90024

Ingle Company, Typographers
11661 San Vicente Blvd., Suite 402
Los Angeles, California 90049

McNaughton & Gunn, Inc., Lithographers
Ann Arbor, Michigan

Cover and Artwork by Cindra B. Dossey

Library of Congress Cataloging-in-Publication Data

Dossey, Donald E., 1934—
  Keying, the power of positive feeling.

  Bibliography: p.
  Includes index.
  1. Neurolinguistic programming — Popular works.
I. Title.
RC489.N47D67   1988   158'.1   89-60820
ISBN Number: 0-925640-00-X   (hard)
ISBN Number: 0-925640-01-8   (soft)

DEDICATION

I dedicate this book to my mother, Elsie, who gave me support when it was beyond anyone else's capacity. Her belief in me, through her words and actions, taught me the true meaning of God.

Rev. Dale Batesole, host of the syndicated T.V. program "There Is A Way" exclaimed, "The response from our viewers is overwhelming each time Dr. Dossey appears on our program!"

Dr. Rollin Smith, veterinarian, writes, "You have expanded my vision. What a major breakthrough!"

Paul Gonzales, WSB-Radio, Atlanta's most popular talk show host, said, "The methods are so easy and quick to learn, Dr. Dossey cures people of anxieties and phobias right over the radio."

Tom Carroll, host of the "Tom Carroll Radio Show", Santa Barbara, California raved, "Dr. Dossey helped me with curing a phobia of mine during a radio interview. He provided me with the concrete tool, Keying, which is a quantum leap in behavioral change."

Janet Wakes, businesswoman wrote, "My separation almost destroyed me. Thanks to your tapes my blood pressure is back to normal and I'm feeling better than I have in years."

Name Withheld, 14 year old, "I never believed I would see my dad off cocaine and alcohol. You have accomplished a great feat."

Gloria Tracy Moss, entertainer, harpist says, "The way you think and teach is the greatest. I'm so glad you have written this book."

TABLE OF CONTENTS

DIAGRAMS, CHARTS AND ACTIVITY SHEETS

ACKNOWLEDGMENTS

Thanks to the many students, patients and seminar participants for the contribution they have made to this book. Without their thirst for knowledge and their faith that change was possible, I would not have been challenged to go beyond the readily available answers for true solutions.

My deepest gratitude is to all of my staff at the Phobia Institute of West Los Angeles. I am thankful for their support and for their being who they are.

My warmest blessings go to Diane Dern at Outcomes Unlimited Press for her trust and love. A special thanks to Cindra Dossey, editor in chief and my liaison to the world in this project. And for Barbara Hart, my special editor, the one who performs miracles, I am truly grateful.

NOTE: Part of the new technology presented in this book was developed through Dr. Dossey's interpretation of some of the innovative techniques of Neuro-Linguistic Programming³ which were developed by John Grinder, Richard Bandler, Leslie Cameron-Bandler, Judith DeLozier, Robert Dilts and David Gordon. These techniques make practical use of systems theory and neuropsychology. Certain words used in this book are neuro-linguistic words of art and are to be construed as Dr. Dossey's understanding of them only.

PREFACE

This book is about fulfillment, change and choice. Happiness and success do not have to belong to "them", the elite five percent. You too can join the ranks of the triumphant five percent. Accomplishment, satisfaction and abundance can also be yours.

This book developed out of my experience in helping people throughout the world overcome anxieties, fears and phobias. It resulted from over two decades of clinical practice and hundreds of motivational and success seminars I have given nationwide.

People who could not travel to the Phobia Institute in West Los Angeles, who could not take advantage of its telephone therapy or attend the seminars wanted a guide to successfully navigate the apparent risky waters of change.

During this time I was barraged with questions. What can I do to be happier and more successful? Why doesn't my therapy seem to be effective? What are the secrets of making the promised results of self-help books and motivational tapes more lasting? What can I do when visualizations and affirmations don't work? These needs motivated me to develop "Through The Briar Patch", an audio cassette program which contains portions of the updated and expanded book you are now reading.

Keying: The Power Of Positive Feelings has been researched not in the quiet halls of institutions, although I taught clinical psychology at a major university for over eight years, but in the bustle of the battlefields of life. This isn't a book of fancy theory; it is a handbook of state-of-the-art specifics. I have used myself, my patients and seminar participants as guinea pigs, refining the craft and sharpening the expertise of predictability. I share with you what works and what doesn't work. It's not just my story, but also the stories of patients, students, and dozens of other happy and prosperous people.

Over the last several years I began to realize that psychotherapy, as generally being practiced, does not work; that positive thinking and holding a positive mental attitude are not measurably predictable: and that motivational approaches are not lasting. However, I also found, that when they are effective, when they do work and do led to success, and when they are lasting, they all have one thing in common — positive feelings. The common denominator to all successful behavior is positive feelings.

All approaches to motivation and success are successful when they generate the necessary feelings. Feelings precede all motivation and behavior. Positive feelings, not thinking, is the immediate precursor to success.

Keying: The Power Of Positive Feelings is about generating the feelings that will lead to happiness, prosperity and peace of mind.

The Keying techniques presented in this book are based on how the brain and body learn best. Keying has been used to wash away anxieties, fears and phobias quickly and permanently. People have used the techniques to increase their self-image, eliminate procrastination, develop instantaneous and lasting motivation. Keying has been demonstrable in increasing prosperity and peace of mind. CHANGE IS NOT ONLY POSSIBLE IT CAN BE FUN, EASY AND PREDICTABLE.

Lives of thousands have been dramatically changed with these revolutionary tools and the results have been published internationally in newspapers and magazines, as well as seen and heard on television and radio around the world.

Now these simple and fun methods are yours. Prepare yourself for the next step beyond positive thinking. Equip yourself for the next step, positive feelings. Brace yourself for the quantum leap.

INTRODUCTION:
THE NEXT GIANT STEP

You did it! You chose to begin a curious, life-changing journey — one that will affect the rest of your life in a positive, powerful way. You are now ready and enthusiastically moving toward a life of more freedom, success, and achievement. Congratulations for taking care of yourself.

This book is about generating changes and creating more choices and control in your life. Human change has been one of the biggest dilemmas in the history of mankind. For thousands and thousands of years people have tried virtually everything to change themselves from the way they are to the way they want to be. And most of the things they tried were not predictably successful. Now, there is a way. You can learn to control the way you feel and take the action you need to achieve your aspirations.

The very act of your reading this page, now, is a statement of your belief that change is possible and that that change will allow you to live a life of freedom, of achievement, and a life of success you perhaps once believed was beyond your wildest dreams.

Sound too good to be true? After years of research and clinical practice it gives me great joy to share with you these revolutionary life-changing discoveries.

Keying: The Power of Positive Feelings gives you concrete explanations and proven techniques. Techniques that will allow you to change the negative habits and behaviors you may have, and to generate new positive habits that will give you the freedom to be what you want to be. You will be able to do all of this quickly and predictably.

WHAT WOULD YOU LIKE TO CHANGE?

What would you like to change? List the changes you desire and with the techniques in this book you can be sure you will make those changes.

Would you like to feel calm, relaxed and alert no matter what you're thinking or what's going on around you? Would you like to be able to feel motivated at will? You'll learn how to do just that.

Would you like to feel confident and capable in any situation? Would you like to be self-assured even in situations that used to make you feel fearful or timid? You will be curiously amazed at the control and power you will have after reading this book. And you will make that power your own.

Would you like to have more love and be more loving? You don't have to wait until that lightening bolt of love hits you. You'll learn how to create loving feelings anytime you want from this dynamic system. In fact you can learn how to have any emotion you want anytime you want to have it, quickly and easily.

How would you like to go through your life free of fear? Free of fear? Free of social fears? Free of relationship fears? Free of fears that keep you from being financially independent? Free of all those nagging fears that limit you? Fears that make you want to pull down the shades, crawl into bed and pull the covers over your head instead of getting out and enjoying life to its fullest? You will learn how to be free of fear from this book.

You may want to free yourself of the negative influences of past trauma. Each one of us has had negative events which took place in the past and the memories and feelings from those experiences still effect our daily lives. They effect our expectations and the way we are in the world. They rob us of energy and joy. You will now learn how to let go of those past negative influences, permanently and effortlessly.

Would you like to stop being shy? Would you like to actually look forward to meeting people, being with people? Would you like to feel comfortable speaking with others? You will learn how to do that with confidence and assurance using your Key and the Keying technique.

Do you want to lose weight or quit smoking or stop any bad habit that's been plaguing you? With your personal Key, you will learn how to change those habits quickly, easily, and permanently.

Would you like to learn how to relax and stay relaxed, wash away stress? You will learn how to do it with ease.

Would you like to be able to set goals so you are always feeling motivated? Do you want to take the necessary actions to get everything you want in life? You will learn precisely how to do that in this book.

The possibilities for your future are virtually limitless.

YOU HAVE WITHIN YOU ALL YOU NEED

You already have, within you, all the resources you need to change what you want to change, to do what you want to do, and to have what you want to have. By getting this book you have already begun to program your unconscious mind to make available the total success you've been looking for. More health, more happiness, more prosperity, and more peace of mind than you have ever imagined is awaiting you!

You were born with positive self-worth. That never changes. Your self-worth is, and always will be, positive. It is only your behavior and reactions that might not be producing the happy and fruitful life you may want. This program does not attempt to change *you*. But, it does allow you to change your own unwanted *behavior* in a safe, easy, and predictable way. You can only succeed. You will discover only positive results and outcomes.

You can now look forward to seeing your problems change into challenging opportunities. And these challenges will become your stepping stones to the fresh, curious, and successful life you deserve!

WHAT IS PERSONAL POWER?

Personal power is having the ability to control your life rather than being controlled by it. That means all areas of your life: your career and financial life, your relationships and social life, and your spiritual life. Personal power is the ability to get and keep control of your life.

Personal power is not abusive, pushy, or coercive power. True personal power is the power that makes you who you really are, the same power that allows you to effect change in the world and in those around you without being offensive or cruel.

THE FIVE PERCENT SOLUTION

It is estimated that only five percent of the population has personal power. Five percent of the population is in control of their lives. Five percent of the population create the results they want. This means that 95 percent of the population does not.

Ninety-five percent of the population has lost control of the circumstances and the results in their lives. Ninety-five percent of the population cannot control their feelings predictably. Ninety-five percent of the population is unhappy, unsatisfied and not living to their fullest potential.

Many of that 95 percent have given up hope of ever realizing their dreams of success, of becoming the way they've dreamed of becoming, or they have given up trying to be as successful as they had dreamed of being. They have simply accepted all this as the way it is. You hear them saying, "This is the way I am, and there's nothing I can do about it."

However, I want to honor you for knowing there is a better way to live and for knowing there is a way to be what you really want to be and to have what you want to have.

I want to applaud you for being so enthusiastic and willing to join the five percent of the population with personal power.

Now what sets this five percent apart? What makes this five percent of successful, powerful people different from the rest?

PERSONAL POWER IS NOT CHANCE OR LUCK

Success or personal power is not the result of chance. From closely studying successful people from all walks of life and people who are successful in a multitude of areas, I've found there are three basic keys to personal power and fruitful living that every successful and powerful person possess.

THREE KEYS TO PERSONAL POWER

The first key is, powerful people can control the way they think. They can control their minds. The second key is, powerful people can control the way they feel. They are in more control of their emotions. And the third key is, powerful and successful people are able to set goals in a specific way and then, by being able to control their feelings, they can take the action necessary to achieve those goals.

Controlling your feelings is the main objective of this book. Controlling your feelings is the major and dominant pivotal point of all personal power. You will be learning how to use these keys, and specifically, controlling your feeling Keys.

You will also clearly understand and use the famous motivation and success formula that will virtually guarantee your success.

YOUR LAST STOP

A few years ago, I founded and directed the Phobia Institute and Stress Management Centers of Southern California. We were treating people from all over the world for fears, stress and depressions. We were treating people who had severe, classically defined phobias like agoraphobia, those who could not leave their homes because of fear, and those who couldn't get into elevators, drive or had the fear of flying, etc. We were, also, treating such social phobias as getting up in front of an audience. But, we were also treating many people who had problems getting ahead financially or maintaining a level of success in their jobs.

I'd like to tell you about one particular person. We'll call him Michael. Michael is typical of many patients who come to see me.

He was 32 years old and had a couple of kids. He was a relatively successful producer and a hard worker.

Michael found he wasn't getting along very well with his wife, his kids, and his co-workers. He was just burned out. No motivation. Unhappy. He was totally locked up inside himself and thought he was losing his mind. He felt a loss of control over his emotions. Michael was also having panic attacks and could not sleep at night. His health had deteriorated.

On top of all this, he was angry and blamed others

for his predicament. All his spirituality was gone. He was even angry at God for not helping him out.

He had tried everything. He had tried psychiatrists, psychologists. He had tried such methods as positive thinking, forceful will power, visualizations, affirmations and subliminal tapes. However, nothing worked.

I told Michael, like I tell everyone who comes to see me, "Michael, this is your last stop. Look, I know your problems seem overwhelming to you now. You seem like you don't have any control. But I want to tell you, your problem is very, very simple."

"You have learned some things" I continued, "that you can unlearn very quickly and you can learn to do something else. And it will happen to you, as you learn the three basic keys to personal power, and particularly, how to control your feelings."

Michael did quickly learn to control his mind, his feelings and his actions and in an easy, effective way. The same way you are learning the techniques in this book.

Michael is now more successful and happier than he's ever been in his life. He's more curious and excited about things. He looks forward to each day as a fresh start with the inquisitiveness and wonder of a child.

Since you are learning the three keys to personal power and specifically, how to control your feelings, to your amazement and surprise, positive changes will be as easy for you as they were for Michael.

These keys are so simple and so profound and they make sense. To be successful you need to know what it is you want and then you have to take the action required to get it. If you can't control how you think and especially how you feel, then you will never be able to do what's necessary to realize your dreams. If you don't have that control, you lose momentum.

You try and you fail. You finally give up and fall back into that 95 percent. How many times have you enthusiastically started a special project, but after a few days or a few weeks you found that you just lost steam? We've all had times like that. But what is it that stopped us? It was the lack of personal power. It was the lack of control over our feelings.

To have more personal power you simply have to be able to set goals and control the way you feel so you can take the essential steps to achieve those goals. It's no mystery. It's actually quite elementary. And you are learning exactly how to do it right now!

THE COMMON DENOMINATOR TO ALL SUCCESS

As a behavior scientist, I have researched numerous motivational psychologies and social success sciences. I have explored an abundance of metaphysical, positive thinking and positive mental attitude approaches. While doing that, I have had the opportunity to analyze various motivational and success oriented best selling books and their philosophies.

I was introduced to authors and books such as Norman Vincent Peale and his famous *Power of Positive Thinking;* Maxwell Maltz' *Psychocybernetics*; Claude M. Bristol's *The Magic of Believing*; Napoleon Hill's *Think and Grow Rich.* — the writings of Og Mandino, Wayne W. Dyer, M.D., Leo Buscaglia, Ph.D, M. Scott Peck, M.D. and others too numerous to mention here.

I have also reviewed many audio and video cassette tape programs on motivation and success. Tapes of such greats as Charles Garfield and his work on "Peak Performance"; Dennis Waitley's "Psychology of Winning"; Earl Nightengale's "Lead the Field"; Zig Ziglar's "Goals: How To Set Them, How To Reach Them". Also, tapes featuring Tom Peters, Lee Iacocoa, Anthony Robins, and many, many more.

In the graduate psychology program at Pepperdine University, I taught all of the psychotherapy and counseling techniques currently being used. There, I had the opportunity to see how they each approached motivation, success and self esteem.

In addition, I studied Science of Mind and its giants like Ernest Holmes, Thomas Troward, Emmett Fox, and their approaches and applications to positive thinking and positive prayer.

With all of these success psychologies, philosophies and approaches I found that sometimes they worked and sometimes they did not work. In fact, I discovered that psychotherapy, positive thinking, visualizing or affirming do not work predictably at all! They are only randomly successful. Recent research has indicated that placebos (sugar pills) and psychotherapy have just about the same effect. At worst, psychotherapy and psychiatry, as they are generally being practiced today, can be hazardous to your emotional and physical health. At best, psychotherapy can be considered love for a fee.

However, with all the myriad of approaches to becoming successful and happy, when they did work, when they were successful they had one thing in common. They all had one overlapping, unifying element in common when they were effective. And that one common denominator is *POSITIVE FEELINGS!*

The one common denominator of every successful method is *positive feelings!* The concepts and frames of mind these methods developed, created positive feelings. *Positive feelings* is the *Common Denominator to Success.* And, the feelings that were created, generated action. Feelings preceded all! behavior!

The promising ideas, the optimistic concepts, the various positive points of view and mental attitudes, when effective, created feelings of faith and hope. And the feelings of faith, created the motivation and action needed to achieve the various goals.

It then became clear to me that, conversely, any negative feelings, emotions or behavior — any form of procrastination or paralyzing inactivity — is due to lack of faith and the absence of the associated motivating physical feeling!

So, I found that positive thinking, visualizations and affirmations (and all of the positive mental attitude approaches) when at all effective, ultimately ended up generating the *feelings* needed that created the desired faith, motivation and successful action! Feelings precede behavior!

Feelings. The common denominator. The overlapping, unifying element to all success, to all movement in life.

Now, this book and the Keying process does not replace positive thinking, visualizing and affirming. Rest assured. you don't have to throw away holding a positive mental attitude or discard prayer. On the contrary, Keying makes them more predictably successful!

No. You don't have to discard positive thinking, your spirituality or your God. After all, they are the very foundation of a rich and rewarding life and the major contribution to humankind. Without a spiritual base we are nothing. This book will not only enrich your relationship with a positive mental attitude but, it will profoundly strengthen your feelings toward your Creator.

THE "DELI SIGN" PHENOMENON — THE SELF FULFILLING PROPHESY

Feelings also relate to a psychological and mental law: the *Self-fulfilling Prophesy*. In the sciences of the mind, the law is called the *Law of Cause and Effect*. I call it the *Deli Sign phenomenon*. That is, when feeling hungry, the unconscious mind fills in the gaps and we automatically begin to see more deli signs and restaurant signs than we normally would!

With a specific success mind/body set — the "as if" *feelings* — trigger the activation of the subconscious and superconscious minds and the powerful intuitive part of us begins to go to work. The unconscious mind fills in the gaps and the Deli Signs of success appear! A seemingly mysterious force comes to our aid and we begin to automatically draw to us the very people, situations and things we need in order to fulfill our dreams!

Dr. Harry Douglas Smith, one of my mentors, and author of *The Secret of Instantaneous Healing* said, "Think as if your life depends upon it, because it does!" That has now been changed to "Think and *FEEL* as if your life depends upon it, because it does!" Feelings precede behavior! Feelings precede faith! Feelings precede motivation and action! Feelings precede success!

THE MOTIVATION AND SUCCESS FORMULA THAT CANNOT FAIL

People with personal power get the results they want by consciously controlling the "THINK/FEEL/DO/HAVE HAVE" MOTIVATION AND SUCCESS FORMULA. The formula is this: "What you think about you begin to feel, and what you feel you begin to do, and what you do determines what you become or have".

Persons not able to get what they want in life, cannot

control the *Think/feel/do/have motivation and success formula*. They get caught in what I call the think/feel — feel/think "fear loop". That is, their negative, self destructive body memories get in their way. They lose control of their feelings. They lose control of the *feel* part of the think/feel/do/have success formula.

However, when successful people *are* successful, *are* able to set goals and stay on track, *are* able to stay focused, then, they can consciously control their feelings, their body memories, the *feel* part of the think/feel/do/have success formula!

Again, feelings is the one common denominator that creates absolutely all of the movement in our lives! Powerful successful positive feelings create faith and motivation.

PSYCHONEUROLINGUISTICS — THE NEXT STEP

Having ascertained that the common denominator to all success is positive feelings, my interests and research then drew me, naturally, toward finding ways to more effectively and predictably control the physical feelings.

I began to study with great interest some linguists and something called *neuro-linguistic programming*™. I was curiously impressed by the work of two men in particular, John Grinder and Richard Bandler, the founders of *neuro-linguistic programming*™. I also researched the work of the legendary medical hypnotist Milton H. Erickson, M.D. who knew that human communication is multi-leveled.

Erickson used certain techniques to tell a seemingly simple story on one level, like a story about tomato plants, and at the same time on another level, he could program a person's phobia to disappear. After he told a variety of multi-leveled stories to his patients, stories about other patients, they found their depressions would lift. Others would start making more money than they had ever made before. Positive changes began to occur.

Milton Erickson's unique story telling approach, and his use of language with patients, was life-altering and made a quantum leap in predictable communication. I studied his work in detail and combined this knowledge with what I had learned about *neuro-linguistic programming*™. I then added my previous knowledge of psychology, communication theory and science of mind.

It was then I began to realize that here was an exciting and extraordinary combination! The proven methods of psychology, linguistics, and the communication sciences could now be meshed with science of mind in a way that would significantly alter the results of behavioral change throughout the world.

This emerging technology is called *psychoneurolinguistics* . This is simply a fancy name for a method of making an impact upon your thoughts, feelings and actions so you can do the things you want.

Psychoneurolinguistics is the most powerful and systematic method known to effect the mind, how you feel, what you do and what you have in your life.

It is important to know that this technology does not attempt to change your belief system, but it does give you the freedom to choose how you want to think and how you want to feel. The very essence of personal power, controlling how you feel.

Suppose you were walking leisurely down the street and a car suddenly came around the corner about to hit you. An appropriate reaction would be feelings of fear. That fear would produce enough adrenaline to help get you out of the way fast. This reaction is imperative to save your life. That fear is appropriate.

But often we have unwanted feelings of fears, just

as automatic but not so useful; such as, phobias and stress or feelings that control our negative habits.

With psychoneurolinguistics, or *PNL*, you will be able to change your unwanted feelings and behavior and achieve more choices and have the success you desire. With those added options comes freedom: freedom from fear, freedom from any negative limitations.

With *PNL* you can have the freedom for more aware-ness, more flexibility. That means you can have more variety of choice in your thinking, feelings, and actions. You will be able to choose success or not.

Let me repeat, *psychoneurolinguistics* is a method; it is not a theory. It is a system of profound methods and techniques that you can use for self-programming and it can be learned in a very systematic, easy, simple and fun way.

This technology is not the Truth, it is simply a way to the Truth.

Psychoneurolinguistics is the next step: the next step in self-understanding, the next step in self-fulfillment. It is the next step in personal and social transformation. It's a step beyond positive thinking, visualizations and affirmation, and a step beyond any motivational course to date.

One of the many procedures found in the science of *psychoneurolinguistics* is Keying. This simple method was originally developed to cure phobias and stress related disorders at the Phobia Institute of West Los Angeles and the Stress Management Centers of South-ern California.

Keying has now been expanded in this book, to include ways of predictably increasing faith, confidence and the motivation necessary to achieve any kind of success!

The Keying processes are now being used to better

physical and mental health, to increase happiness, to insure more financial security and peace of mind! YOU NEVER HAVE TO HAVE ANOTHER BAD DAY!

WHAT IS A "KEY" AND WHAT IS "KEYING"?

A Key (and the Keying process) is simply a conscious use of what is actually going on all the time. Natural keying is a stimulus that produces all of our moods, emotions, and actions usually without our even being aware of it.

Simply put, a Key is a purposefully created button, which when consciously pushed, will give you any feelings you want, automatically, in two to seven seconds. It is a major breakthrough in the science of behavioral change.

A Key is a predetermined stimulus that you can consciously use to lock in and unlock any feelings or unconscious body memories you want!

Keying is a predictable *technique* with which you can lock in or unlock any feelings you want regardless of what you are thinking or what is going on around you. The Key is the thing, and Keying is the method.

Keying is easily learned. It bypasses the analytical thought processes. It can be used to permanently wash away fears and phobias, as well as any negative, unwanted feelings associated with any past experience.

More profoundly, Keying is a simple and systematic way to create the necessary feelings for success, to consciously maintain and use these motivating feelings when desired, and to easily recall these action producing body memories when needed to virtually guarantee your achieving your dreams!

Keying is fast and measurable. With Keying you will be able to have a positive, purposeful and potent influence on your world and those in it. You can now have unlimited success!

While using these methods to treat severely phobic and depressed patients, I noticed quick, permanent results. I was able to use these techniques to wash away stress and stress related disorders. Then I detected something more.

I discovered that patients who learned these techniques, began to automatically develop more personal power and began to have more control over their lives! These people who generated more personal power had more success, just like those people who were already successful.

I then began to teach people how to model excellence. In other words, I began teaching people how to use what you, and others, have already done successfully and then, how to transfer that to other areas where they might be lacking.

Now, *Keying: The Power Of Positive Feelings* will make this knowledge available to you in a simplified form. This is the most incredible program in existence. It is a major innovation in the behavior sciences and a quantum leap in predictability.

HOW IS THIS BOOK DIFFERENT?

What makes *psychoneurolinguistics* and Keying specifically, so dramatically different is that the results are predictable and measurable. And, they are fun and easy to learn. Look forward to the positive, permanent changes that are perhaps occurring in your life right now. And again, have fun!

HOW TO USE THIS BOOK

Research has shown that for quicker and better results, first simply thumb through your book looking at the chapters in sequence. You can do this all at once, or in shorter blocks of time, it doesn't matter. The important thing is to do it in sequence.

After you have leafed through the book, write down what you want to get from reading your book. You may want to list your desired changes on the page titled, "What I Want To Get From This Book".

After listing your desired changes, begin again, stopping to do your self-programming activities when instructed to do so. This book, like my audio cassette tapes, is scientifically designed to make an impact on your unconscious as well as your conscious mind. Because of the linguistic structures and what may sometimes appear to be redundancies, by simply reading this book you will begin to undergo noticeable, measurable positive changes.

As you do the activities, your unconscious mind and body memories will assimilate the material and you will begin to receive enormous and beneficial results. Your activities can be referred to repeatedly in any order you prefer for further reinforcement.

Your activities are also scientifically fashioned to aid you in your mastery of the techniques. There is no right way or wrong way to do them. You can do them as you read. You can do them alone or with someone. You can read them into a tape recorder and play them back. It doesn't matter. Your unconscious mind doesn't know the difference. You can only succeed. What does matter is to start.

Remember, because of way in which the technology and the techniques in your program work, you are

WHAT I WANT TO GET FROM THIS BOOK

Mental and/or Intellectual Goals: Desired Completion Date

_____

_____

_____

Emotional Goals:

_____

_____

_____

Physical Goals:

_____

_____

_____

Financial Goals and Work-related Goals:

_____

_____

_____

Social and Relationship Goals:

_____

_____

_____

Spiritual Goals:

_____

_____

_____

(If you need more space, use additional paper)

already beginning to get focused and are now ready to reach heights of success of which you may have only dreamed!

TO GET STARTED

To get a good start, answer these questions.

Do I want to get more control of my feelings and my life? Do I want to learn how to predictably create the necessary feelings I need for success? Do I want to consciously maintain and use these motivating feelings when I desire? Do I want to be able to systematically and easily recall these unconscious action producing body memories when I need them?.

If you answered "Yes" to any or all of these questions, then *Keying: The Power of Positive Feelings* is the book for you. The Keying process has been measurably proven to get positive thinking, affirmations and visualizations to work more predictably! It is a revolutionary quantum leap in controlling your feelings.

This book will explain the powerful Keying technique. It will cover how the successfully proven Keying process was discovered and how random and purposeful Keys are being experienced consciously or unconsciously every minute of our lives.

You will learn how you can create and use your own powerful feeling Keys and, like thousands of others, get all of the happiness, love, prosperity and joy you want.

You will discover ways to go beyond positive thinking, beyond visualizations and affirmations into the realm of ultimate power — the power of positive feelings.

You will be able to predictably and measurably take control of a profound and proven motivation and success formula that will enhance all areas of your life. You will learn amazingly failproof, step-by-step ways to take total control of your feelings and your life once and for all!

In the back of your book you will find my "Fear and Phobia Finder". It is to assist you in locating and identifying over 250 fears and phobias, the most common unwanted habits and the various blocks and barriers to success. Once identified, you are given change strategies in a step-by-step cookbook approach to best handle these challenging opportunities in the most profound, pervasive and lasting way.

Also in the Appendices, you'll find powerful "Daily Affirmations" to deepen the learnings found in this book. These frames of mind or points of view are assumptions successful and happy people hold and with which they approach their world.

Focusing on these affirmations and holding the related feelings for 30 days makes the attainment of success a guarantee.

Have you ever noticed the wonder and excitement a small child has for some of the simplest pleasures in life? That pure curiosity and thrill for life and what it brings will be yours as you read this book. You will be able to think the way you want to think, feel the way you want to feel, any time, any place, no matter what is going on around you. You will be able to set goals and achieve the results you want. You too, will begin to recapture that curiosity and wonder. Your own personal power will begin to increase to your amazement and surprise.

YOUR GUARANTEE TO COMPLETE SUCCESS

The only thing left to do is to commit to yourself to begin and commit to stick with it. The only way you can fail is if you don't start or if you start and then quit.

Geothe wrote the following poem:

COMMITMENT

"Until one is committed
  there is hesitancy, the chance to draw back,
  always ineffectiveness.

Concerning all acts of initiative and creation,
  there is one elementary truth,
  the ignorance of which kills countless ideas
  and splendid plans:
  that the moment one definitely commits oneself,
  then Providence moves too.

All sorts of things occur to help one
  that would never otherwise have occurred.

A whole stream of events issues from the decision
  raising in one's favor all manner
  of unforeseen incidents and meetings
  and material assistance,
  which no man could have dreamt
  would have come his way.

Whatever you can do, or dream you can, begin it.
  Boldness has genius, power, and magic in it."

Thank you. I will see you on the road of abundance and joy. Have a curious and exciting journey!

CHAPTER I.

MAKING THE "IMPOSSIBLE" POSSIBLE

HOW WOULD YOU LIKE TO BE ABLE TO:

FEEL THE WAY YOU WANT TO ALWAYS;

CREATE POWERFUL FEELINGS OF FAITH, LOVE, CREATIVITY, OR CONFIDENCE ON COMMAND;

UNLOCK BLOCKS AND BARRIERS THAT ARE KEEPING YOU FROM DOING WHAT YOU KNOW YOU CAN DO;

LOCK OUT PAINFUL FEELINGS ASSOCIATED WITH THE PAST;

CREATE AND LOCK IN ANY FEELINGS YOU WANT FOR ANY FUTURE SITUATION;

WASH AWAY FEARS, PHOBIAS, AND STRESS FOREVER;

CREATE INSTANTANEOUS MOTIVATION;

ACHIEVE ALL THE HEALTH, HAPPINESS, LOVE, PROSPERITY, AND PEACE OF MIND YOU WANT AND DESERVE?

Does all this seem too impossible to attain? Before we learn the specific Keying techniques, let's look at some ideas that perhaps will help us realize we can have our dreams fulfilled. Then we'll do some activities, in addition to the ones in the Introduction, that will perhaps prove to us how we can make the *impossible become possible.*

We were born with certain automatic unconscious activities that, when consciously used, can serve to assist us in attaining and maintaining a chosen level of success. One activity is how the unconscious mind fills in the gaps. The other, I call the Deli Sign phenomenon. These unconscious operations can be consciously and purposefully used to powerfully influence your feelings and your behavior.

USING THE UNCONSCIOUS MIND TO FILL IN THE GAPS

Before you go any farther, look at the drawing entitled "Fill in the Gaps" and write down your first impressions.

What did you see on the "Fill in the Gaps" page? A lot of people see a square. Some see a box. Others see a house. However, if you look very closely you'll notice it's really only four lines, not touching each other and not very neatly drawn either. What happened? Your unconscious mind filled in the gaps. That's an automatic function of the unconscious mind.

That's why by acquiring and reading this book and setting up your goals, your unconscious mind is *already* filling in the gaps!

Since research has proven that our unconscious mind controls 99 percent of our behavior, that's the mind we want to learn to influence — the *unconscious mind.* (The *unconscious mind, subconscious mind* and *body*

FILL IN THE GAPS

WHAT IS THIS?

(Write down your first impressions)

_____

_____

_____

_____

Now continue reading to find out the answer.

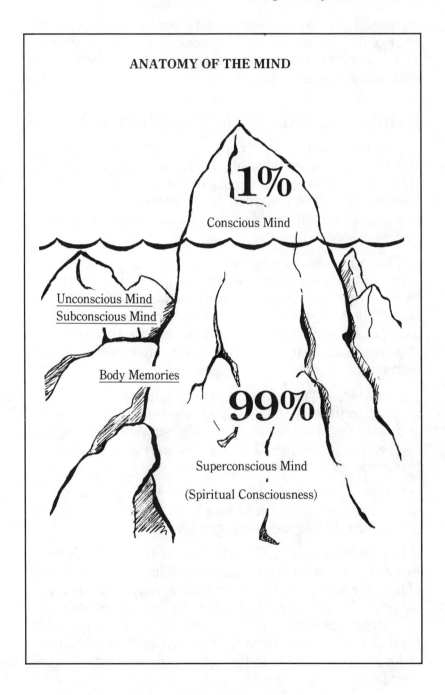

ANATOMY OF THE MIND

1%

Conscious Mind

Unconscious Mind
Subconscious Mind

Body Memories

99%

Superconscious Mind

(Spiritual Consciousness)

memories are all the same thing and are used interchangeably in this book.) This book is teaching you new and powerful ways to very easily and specifically control your *unconscious mind*.

USING THE "DELI SIGN" PHENOMENON

The other activity used in controlling your mind is the Deli Sign phenomenon. Perhaps you can recall a time when you got a sensation in your body called hunger, and all of a sudden you became aware of more deli signs, restaurant signs and cafe signs than you had ever seen before.

That process is also an automatic, unconscious operation of your body and your mind. It is important to note that the deli signs were *already there. Already there!* The *body/mind set* we call hunger, begins to create a conscious and unconscious awareness for those things that will satisfy it. Suddenly, you're aware of the deli signs.

Likewise, if you create a strong success body/mind set, the *feelings* of success, you will automatically and suddenly become aware of all the success Deli Signs — the things, people, ideas, etc. *already there* that will bring you your success.

Create a love body/mind set and you are automatically attracted to love and love is attracted to you. Like begets like. Water seeks its own level.

In psychology, it's called the Law of the Self-fulfilling Prophecy. In other mind sciences, it is called the Law of Cause and Effect. Based on your body/mind set, that is, your thoughts and *feelings*, your unconscious mind will automatically fill in the gaps and your desires will begin to be drawn to you. You will perceive reality tailored to your specific thoughts and feelings — your specific body/mind set.

It is important to remember that your unconscious mind fills in the gaps and organizes how you perceive things, based not so much on the outside world, but rather on your world inside, your thoughts and feelings. Your internal creates the external.

With your Keying process you will learn how to create various body/mind sets that will enable your unconscious mind to fill in the gaps and automatically organize the world around you in accordance with your desires. You will begin to see the Deli Signs of your dreams in all areas of your life; health, financial, relationships, career. Remember, they are already there!

Your own powerful feeling Key will give you the ability to create your own body/mind set and to set up your goals so specifically, so profoundly that your unconscious mind will automatically generate the action necessary for you to achieve and truly enjoy your dreams.

This book makes all this available to you. It offers you predictable and measurable techniques that will allow you to do what mankind has always dreamed of — making positive and conscious, systematic choices that will lead to your fulfillment and success.

Imagine the results. You will have better health, a more rewarding social life, the financial status that you've always wanted to have and more. You are going to learn to use the three basic keys to personal power, the three basic keys to controlling your thoughts, your feelings and your actions.

You are going to become a member of the elite five percent. Those who have success, who have power, and who have satisfaction and fulfillment in their lives. You can say good-bye to the 95 percent for the rest of your life! Enjoy yourself as you learn, and remember, your unconscious mind is filling in the gaps *and* look for the Deli Signs along the way!

MAKING THE "IMPOSSIBLE" EVEN MORE POSSIBLE!

You may still be wondering if this all sounds a little too good to be true. You might even have some doubts about getting what you want in life and doing it the way you'd like to. I know I certainly did at first exposure to these ideas and methods. However, the successful experience of thousands has certainly given me a completely new perspective on making the "impossible" become possible.

Perhaps you can think back to when you were a very small child. You may have thought it impossible to learn to turn on a light. But you did it, and you now take it for granted. At one point in your life you may have found the idea of riding a bicycle quite impossible. That too, you mastered and now do it without even thinking.

What about driving a car? Just about every pre-teen is concerned whether he or she will ever learn to drive a car in heavy traffic. Impossible! Yet it happened. The "impossible" again becomes possible!

You can now consciously make those things possible that you once felt were absolutely impossible to achieve.

The following activity helps me and perhaps it can help you too.

Turn to the page entitled "First Thought Impossible — Now Possible". Do the activities listed. Remember, you don't have to be perfect in these techniques. Your unconscious mind will fill in the gaps.

Your unconscious mind controls 99 percent of your functioning. Just imagine what would happen if you could program in a specific goal and simply allow *both* your conscious and your unconscious minds to organize information in a way that would assist you in obtaining your dreams!

FIRST THOUGHT IMPOSSIBLE — NOW POSSIBLE

Purpose: To help you realize that you *can* accomplish the "Impossible"

Write three examples from your life of things you thought were *impossible* for you to *do* or have that are *now possible* and *easy* for you. For example, riding a bike or swimming.

As you do this, perhaps you will begin to realize the unlimited possibilities and resources you have within you.

1. _____

_____

2. _____

_____

3. _____

_____

The "impossible" can become possible. Think of how your life would be different if you had a way to consciously and predictably control your feelings. The "impossible" can become possible. Right now is the ideal time to begin the practice of thinking in terms of making the "impossible" possible!

GOING BEYOND YOUR LIMITS

Let's do another simple activity that will give you an even stronger sense of the power I've been talking about. That way, you can get an idea of how you are going to be able to go beyond your limits with the techniques in this book. You can then more easily make possible what was first apparently impossible.

First of all, I'd like you to stand up. (Do this activity as you read if you can, or you can read the activity, put the book down and do it. You can have someone read it to you as you do it. It doesn't matter). Stand up and then slowly raise both arms, straight out to your sides, until they are parallel with the floor, palms down. Then, turn your head to your right so that your eyes are following your right arm down to the end of your fingers.

Point with your right hand and slowly begin to turn your arms, head and upper body to the right. Keep your feet flat on the floor. Turn now as far as you can to the right. Now hold that position for a moment, and with your eyes make an imaginary line from the end of your finger to a point on the wall. Twist as far as you can and mark an imaginary spot on the wall. Okay. Now slowly come back and slowly lower your arms. Let them hang by your sides and relax.

Now I want you to close your eyes and *imagine only*, keeping your body as it is, and keeping your hands to your sides, just imagine that you are raising your arms again, holding them out to the sides, parallel to the floor, just as before.

Now see, in your mind's eye, yourself turning to the right, just as you did before, farther and farther to the right, looking down your right arm to the end of your right finger. Imagine you are going close to that spot that you saw on the wall before. Now, imagine yourself going *beyond* that spot on the wall. Imagine yourself going way beyond that spot until you almost *feel* a little tension in the body from pulling so far beyond that spot. In your imagination — go *way beyond* that spot.

Now slowly imagine yourself coming back to the original position and slowly lower your arms. Relax. Now open your eyes.

Okay. Now actually raise your arms again, in the same position as before and slowly turn to the right. Turn as far as you can go. And now, notice how far you can go. Isn't that amazing? The astonishing thing about that activity is with simply your imagination and a little bit of *feeling* in your body, you are able to go beyond your originally perceived limits in a very short period of time.

This is exactly how the various methods you're going to learn are going to work for you. You will be able to shoot beyond your believed limits. You will be able to surpass your wildest expectations in terms of experiencing and having what you want. And keep in mind, you'll do it just as easily and as effortlessly as you did when you went beyond your limits just now in the going beyond your limits activity.

Now let's go on to the next chapter, "The Body/ Mind Connection". There you will discover how we learn, how you can use a scientifically proven motivation and success formula, and a way to frame the mind that will virtually guarantee success!

CHAPTER II.

THE BODY/MIND CONNECTION:

THE POWER OF THE THINK/FEEL/DO/ HAVE SUCCESS FORMULA

Let's talk a little more about body/mind and just how the body and the mind interrelate. I don't want to get too technical, I just want to build a model of how you think and why you feel the way you feel. This will further help you understand how your thinking sets off an automatic chain reaction that creates what you do and what you have. I call this formula the *Think-Feel-Do-Have Motivation and Success Formula*.

THE THINK/FEEL/DO/HAVE MOTIVATION AND SUCCESS FORMULA

The first thing in understanding and using the think-feel-do-have motivation and success formula is to realize the outside world *does not* create your feelings. The outside world *does not* create your moods or your actions. Rather, it's *how* you think about what is going on outside that creates how you *feel* and consequently what you *do.* It's how you see those internal pictures or how and what you say to yourself with that internal self talk that causes those feelings. It's how you *think about* what's going on in the outside world that causes your feelings and your actions. And you've simply *learned* to think the way you think.

It is basically very simple. What you think about you begin to feel. What you begin to feel you begin to do. And what you do, you begin to have or you tend to become. That, in a nut shell, is the think-feel-do-have success formula.

For example, think of somebody you really like. I mean, really like. Do that right now. Notice how you feel. Then, think of somebody you don't like and notice how that feels.

I'm sure you can begin to realize how you would probably act differently with the person you like as opposed to the person you don't like. All because of how you *feel.* And what caused the feelings? What you were thinking. Remember, it's not what happens in the outside world that creates your feelings. It's *how and what you think about* what happens in the world that creates your feelings.

It boils down to this: how you think determines the kind of feelings you have and these feelings determine the kind of action you take. The think-feel-do-have formula is the basic way every human being functions all the time. This process produces every result we have in our lives.

When we use it randomly, unconsciously, we get random, haphazard results. But when we learn to consciously control the think-feel-do-have process we can produce any results we want predictably, measurably and easily.

THE DOSSEY MOTIVATION
AND SUCCESS FORMULA

THINK   FEEL   DO   HAVE

WHAT YOU THINK ABOUT, YOU BEGIN TO FEEL . . .
WHAT YOU FEEL, YOU BEGIN TO DO . . .
WHAT YOU DO, DETERMINES WHAT
YOU HAVE OR BECOME.

YOU WERE BORN WITH ONLY TWO EMOTIONS AND ONLY TWO FEARS

It is interesting to know that each of us is born with only *two basic emotions*. One is love, and the other is fear. And each of us is born with only *two fears*. One is the fear of falling and the other is the fear of loud noises. And that's it. From those two emotions and from only those two fears, everything else we fear or do is learned. Everything.

You were not born with negative thinking or a negative self-image. You were not born with self-destructive habits. You were not born with the fear of failure. You were not born with the fear of going into elevators or the fear of relationships. *All* of your fears and any other fear or negative behavior you may have, *you have learned*. This is quite obvious, yet ever so important to understand.

All of the things that limit any of us, we have simply learned. It might be fear of success, bad habits, shyness, loneliness or the lack of motivation. They are all learned.

Each of us needs to acknowledge our problems, yet we can also understand that no negative behavior or habit is set in concrete. What you have learned you can unlearn. You can replace fear and negativity with new positive habits or behavior. In fact, you are doing it right now as you read this book.

HOW WE LEARN

There are only three basic ways we learn. We learn from *intense feelings*, from *repetition*, and from *modeling*. All of these, by the way, involve a process called *stimulus-response*.

A stimulus causes a response. There is always a cause and then an effect. There is always a stimulus and then a response. We cannot not respond and we cannot not have a stimulus. And, except for fearing loud noises and falling, we learn everything from intense feelings, repetition, and/or modeling.

INTENSE FEELINGS

Let's take trauma for example. We stick our finger in the hot stove, it burns, so we pull it out. From that one trial learning, from that one *intense experience*, we learn to never place our finger onto the hot stove again. The same thing goes for people who have had an automobile accident. Often, from that one experience, the one trauma, they'll never go into an automobile again. They will have a phobia.

Trauma or an *intense feeling,* actually engraves nerve pathways into the body, or neurological tracks, deep into the unconscious mind, creating what is called body memories or muscle memories.

Body memories are patterns of thoughts and feelings that are stored in the physiology and muscles of the body and they can result from just one traumatic or intense experience.

These painful, fearful memories can be triggered, or retrieved, automatically by the same stimulus or one similar to it. In other words, after an accident, a person might go up to an automobile or simply think about the automobile, or any automobile, and this may trigger his learned body memories of fear. It will often create the panic feelings or feelings similar to the first experience that the person had at the time of the accident. Remember, the unconscious mind fills in the gaps — positive or negative.

REPETITION AND REHEARSAL

Another way we learn is from *repetition* or *rehearsal*; that is, as we do something over and over again in the same way. Through repetition, we learned how to tie our shoes, get dressed, drive a car. Through repetition and rehearsal, we again deepen those learned body memories, those thought/feeling patterns, those neurological pathways in our unconscious, until they become automatic.

MODELING OR COPYING

The third way we learn is through what is called *modeling*. We learned by copying or modeling our parents or people around us. That's why so many of us have often become like those around us. The modeling process also creates deep unconscious neurological tracks or body memories.

That's why, in my audio cassette program "Through The Briar Patch," I tell people who want to be successful in any endeavor, to hang around people who have already done what they want to do. The modeling process works at a deep unconscious level.

All three of these modes of learning: intense feeling, repetition and modeling tie into the *think-feel-do-have success formula*. What we learn will determine what we think, feel and do, which in turn, determines our ability to be and stay successful.

If you find yourself addicted to any negative process, remember, you learned it. However, with the techniques you are learning you can easily unlearn it. You can change that pattern. You can replace it with a positive and successful one.

You perhaps are now discovering the staggering importance of the think-feel-do-have motivation and success formula. "What you think about, you begin to feel and what you feel, you begin to do and what you do, determines what you have."

BREAKING THE "FEAR LOOP" AND THE "FEAR CHAIN"

Let's look again at the think-feel-do-have formula. This time from inside the formula — the think-feel part.

You'll notice that how and what you think creates your feelings *and* what you feel, can also, determine what you think, like a loop. It is a very simple loop. It goes like this, "What you think about, you begin to feel, and what you feel, you begin to think about." You can, also, easily get caught in what I call the *fear loop*, the *think-feel — feel-think* fear loop. The simple stimulus-response process goes into a cycle and you can't get out.

For example, if you think of a fearful thought, that creates a fearful feeling. Then the fearful feeling causes more fearful thoughts and a loop occurs. A chain reaction occurs in which one triggers off the other and it's difficult to get out.

You are usually not taught a way to break out of the loop or how to find an exit point. Usually, you can't move into the do or have part of the think-feel-do-have motivation and success formula because you are caught in that think-feel — feel-think loop. When you are caught in that loop, you have literally lost control of your mind. Now remember, you have not lost your mind. You have lost *control* of your mind. You have simply lost your ability to get out of those big, looming, negative mental pictures. You have lost the ability to push those pictures away and disassociate or disengage yourself from to control the loud volume of those negative thoughts or that negative self-talk.

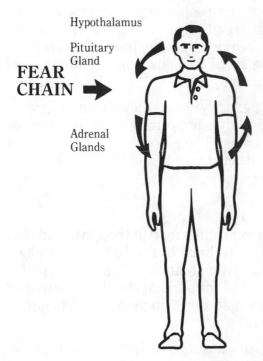

THE "FEAR LOOP"

Think/Feel-Feel/Think

Hypothalamus

Pituitary
Gland

**FEAR
CHAIN** ➡

Adrenal
Glands

More importantly, you have also lost control of your bodily feelings. That is, those body memories are so strong you lose the ability to stay calm and relaxed or motivated regardless of what you are thinking or what's going on around you. With the loss of control of the bodily feelings, you also lose the ability to get in and out of those mental pictures. You get caught up in them and the cycle starts all over again.

I have heard so many people say, "Dr. Dossey, I am just overwhelmed. I can't get on top of things. My problems seem too heavy to handle. It's as if everything is coming down on me. I feel down in the dumps and I can't get a grip on things."

They are saying exactly what they mean. They are literally describing what is happening inside their minds and inside their bodies. Their bodies feel so bad they have lost control of their feelings and their lives.

FEAR CHAIN

Now, when a person thinks fearful thoughts and they begin to feel negative feelings in the body, a fear chain gets activated. This fear chain is when the hypothalamus, the pituitary and the adrenal glands are activated and send adrenaline and other high voltage chemicals throughout the body.

When this happens a surge of fear is experienced. You may recognize this as a sudden sensation of butterflies in your stomach, a hot, flushing face, a racing heart or other unusual feelings of stress. *Stress* and *fear* chemically and physiologically are exactly the same thing! Regardless of what the stressor is, stress prepares the body for flight, fight, or freeze.

Fear *also* prepares the body to run, to attack, or to freeze, just like stress. Your body cannot distinguish the difference. Adrenaline and the stress feelings trigger the next round of negative thoughts. The process has now become that automatic loop again.

THE ADDICTION TO UNHAPPINESS

The process has also become habituated. You become literally *addicted* to the negative feelings. Addicted to those high voltage chemicals and addicted to the process like any addict. Not that you like it or want it. I don't believe any addict ever wants to take that next drink, or pop the next pill but they've lost control. And when you're addicted to fear and stress, you've lost control. Anytime you are caught in the think-feel — feel-think fear loop, you have lost control of your mind and lost control of your feelings.

And to complicate matters even more, the activation of the immune system in the body slows down or shuts off. That means there are fewer white blood cells in the body and the viruses and germs can enter your body more easily. Then you are more susceptible to disease.

Also the endorphins, nature's analgesic morphine-like pain relievers are reduced in number. You may get tired quickly. You might ache all over and you are more prone to physical, mental and social breakdown. And remember, what you feel you begin to think.

It sounds overwhelming, I know, but take heart and have faith. You can learn ways to break these negative cycles. You can learn to control your mind and your body. As a result you will soon find yourself in complete control of your life with an extraordinary future awaiting you!

TRYING TOO HARD DOESN'T WORK

Let's make some other observations about the body-mind and see how they relate to the think-feel-do-have success formula.

The first one is trying too hard does not work. In the mind and the body, when you *try too hard*, you create *resistance* and generally failure.

Very often in my seminars I'll have a person come out in front of the audience. I'll have them hold their hand out and I'll then push against it and they'll push back. When I pull their arm toward me, they pull it back away from me. These opposite responses are automatic unconscious responses. I do not ask them to react the way they do.

What happens in our minds and in our bodies is this, "a push gets a push and a pull gets a pull." For example, when you are talking to someone and you push them by saying, "I don't want you to, I don't want you to!" they will usually push back and say, "But I want to, I want to!" And conversely, when you pull at someone real hard and say, "I want you to, I want you to!" they will pull away and say, "I don't want to, I don't want to!"

A push gets a push and a pull gets a pull. And when you try too hard either way, a resistance is set up which is called a *polarity response*. You'll want to remember this when you start purposefully using the think-feel-do-have success formula. Because if you try too hard or you push or pull too hard to get the results you want, you may create unnecessary resistance to being able to do what you want in the quickest and easiest way.

PINK ELEPHANT EXPERIMENT

Let's do an experiment. Just reach down and grab your left knee, and as you grab your knee, don't think "pink elephant." Oops, too late, now you are going to have a "pink elephant" on that knee for a long time! But it's a harmless pink elephant, so you can relax.

Let's analyze what just happened. In order to make

sense out of the statement, "Don't think pink elephant," you had to think pink elephant. And remember, what you think you begin to feel and do.

So the rule is this: what follows a "don't" or any negative is going to be obeyed consciously, unconsciously and behaviorally. It will be obeyed, just like a strong hypnotic command. And again, what you think about, you begin to feel; and what you feel, you begin to do; and what you do, you tend to have.

Keep this in mind when you find yourself thinking negatively and say, "Oops! I don't want to think negatively . . ." Or when you start saying things like, "I don't want to be depressed or I don't want to feel bad." Or "I don't want to be poor or I don't want to blow this job." What you are doing is programming yourself to feel, do, and have the very thing that you don't want. And you may not even know it. So remember, "don'ts" don't work!

GOING BEYOND YOUR "COMFORT ZONE"

Another phenomenon that keeps people stuck is called the *comfort zone*.

Have you ever wondered why some people inherit or win a fortune and end up losing it or becoming ill? What is it about those who can't seem to hang onto love or happiness? Have you seen people who seem to be addicted to poverty or mediocrity or unhappiness?

Have you ever wondered why some enormously successful people commit acts of reckless self destruction? We can all think of a movie star who ended her life in her prime. Celebrities, business magnates, even presidents have been known to destroy their lives in what the world saw as the most successful time in their lives.

All of these questions and issues allude to a phenomenon called the comfort zone.

The comfort zone is not necessarily comfortable or desirable. It is a zone that keeps us boxed in or locked up in a limiting way. The comfort zone is a zone of feelings or sensations in our bodies which keeps us limited psychologically, physically and/or socially. It is a level which prevents us from attaining the success we may want. Curiously enough, it can keep many of us from attaining success or even keeping success once we get it.

The comfort zone is a level of feelings in the body within which you feel familiar, comfortable, at home with or relaxed. Most importantly, you are free of tense feelings. The comfort zone is not necessarily comfortable in the sense of being satisfied or of having luxury. Rather it is comfortable in the sense of having the minimum of uncomfortable tension in your body.

Anything you do that increases the feeling in your body beyond the comfort zone, even if it's a positive feeling, can often make you do something to get back to that safe level of familiar comfort, even if you have to give up what you wanted most!

Can you remember a time when you went on a diet, lost the weight you wanted to lose, looked good, and then found yourself slowly gaining all of that weight back again? The comfort zone phenomenon is why so many diets and exercise programs don't work or they don't last.

You may truly want to do these things, but when you start to attain your goal and when you find that your dieting takes you out of your familiar comfort zone, you'll generally have to do something to get back to where you feel more comfortable or where it's at least familiar. This is not unusual.

THE COMFORT ZONE

UNCHANGED COMFORT ZONE
The limited, usual, familiar range of tolerable feelings
in the body ("good" or "bad").

GOOD FEELINGS

COMFORT ZONE ·

BAD FEELINGS

EXPANDED COMFORT ZONE
(After setting Outcome frame and Keying)

When the Comfort Zone is expanded we are able to
tolerate more good feelings in our bodies. Notice that
even the worse feelings are better than before when the
Comfort Zone is expanded.

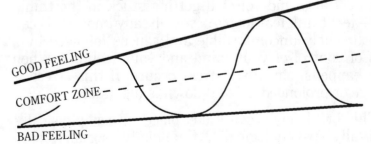

GOOD FEELING

COMFORT ZONE

BAD FEELING

Most people simply will not tolerate feeling better or worse than their comfort zones will allow. Like most people, you may find you will do something in order to get back into your comfort zone. Even if that means sabotaging your success or happiness, you will probably do it. You will most likely do anything to get back into that narrow area where you feel free of tension.

The comfort zone phenomenon is often the reason so many doctors pull their hair out when patients won't take their prescriptions. It is the same phenomenon that renders psychotherapies, motivational talks and pop psychologies ineffective or the results, at best, short lived.

In my research, I have found, unless there is some intervention made, that when a person becomes more successful than they are accustomed, they will begin to consciously, unconsciously or behaviorally destroy the very thing they have worked so hard to accomplish. Somewhere, deep inside, they want to get back to that feeling level they are accustomed to. Those body memories they're familiar with. They want to move back into their comfort zone.

SIGN POSTS OF FEAR AND STRESS

Anytime you start stepping out of your comfort zone, you may also find yourself getting stuck in the think-feel—feel-think fear loop. As you already know, this can be extremely uncomfortable and can be followed by a loss of control of your mind and your feelings. When this happens, obviously stress occurs. If this stress is severe or prolonged, a breakdown is inevitable.

The breakdown can take place either physically, mentally, psychologically, financially, socially, spiritually, or a combination of any or all of these. You may want to find a page entitled "Signposts of

SIGNPOSTS OF FEAR AND STRESS
(A Partial List)

PHYSICAL	EMOTIONAL/MENTAL	SOCIAL/WORK RELATED (FINANCIAL)
Rashes	Uncontrollable, racing thoughts	Procrastination
Hives	Fearful Images — larger than life	Getting and losing jobs, relationships, etc.
Ulcers	Negativism	Excessive arguing
Migraine Headaches	Loud thoughts of doom and disaster	Excessive jealousy
Muscle stiffness	Anxieties	Spiteful behavior
Body pains	Shyness	Addictive love relationships
Digestive problems	Fears	Work slow-downs
Elimination problems	Phobias	Excessive need to control
Heart palpitations	Panic Attacks	Need to be controlled
Hypertension	Fear of losing control	Accident proneness
Rapid or irregular breathing	Irritability, whining, blaming others for problems	
Hyperactivity	Anger/Rage	Self-destructive behavior
Fatigue	Delusions	Quitting jobs
Alcoholism	Depression	Compulsive behavior
Substance abuse	Self-Image Distortions	Abandonment of families
Insomnia	Disorientation	Lack of motivation
Backaches	Irrational thoughts and behavior	Procrastination
Heart Attack	Hallucinations	Poor reality testing
Cancer	Suicidal/Homicidal thoughts	Withdrawal

Fear and Stress" to get a clearer idea of what can happen.

A WAY OUT

Until the recent research in *psychoneurolinguistics*, and Keying specifically, no predictable methods to get people out of these horrible and difficult problems even existed. But with the techniques you are learning, you will be able to expand your comfort zone safely, and easily. *Psychoneurolinguistics* is giving you the tools you can take with you and use for the rest of your life.

These tools will free you from dependency on psychotherapists, teachers, gurus, or the latest self-help book with quick but temporary fixes. You can now be free from dependency on drugs to get you through those rough times. Finally, predictable, permanent and powerful solutions are available.

The way out of all of your problems is exactly the way you got into them: through learning. You've become the way you are by using the think-feel-do-have formula unconsciously and now you are making the wise choice of using this same formula both consciously and unconsciously.

Imagine the power that will be yours as you learn to put into use the think-feel-do-have formula systematically and purposefully. The satisfaction and joy you seek is now coming to you. With the techniques you are learning, you can look forward to the positive, powerful results that you have always wanted.

THE POWER OF "FRAMING"

One of the most powerful means to success is called *Framing*

I am excited to talk to you now about *Framing* and

the *Outcome Frame*. This concept is one of the major secrets to the power of the think-feel-do-have motivation and success formula. If you learn nothing else in this entire book except how to use the Outcome Frame, the beneficial results in your life will be staggering.

What is a Frame? A Frame is a frame of mind — a point of view. A Frame is the way you think about a problem or a goal; your perspective; your focus; your attitude; how you look at things.

Let's say you have a tremendous fear of flying, and you must take a flight to Los Angeles the next morning. Just thinking about the flight makes you terrified. Your fear of flying is overwhelming, because you're focusing on a frame of mind which produces the problem, those negative feelings. What you think about you begin to feel.

What's the alternative? Reframe. Reframe your thoughts. Instead of focusing on those negative thoughts in the problem frame, thoughts that produce negative feelings, you can clearly define your desired outcome and focus on that. In this case, you want a smooth, calm and safe flight. You want to feel calm and relaxed perhaps.

You can reframe your *Problem Frame* into an *Outcome Frame*. Then, specific positive thoughts will produce those positive feelings you want instead.

When creating an Outcome Frame, you want to be sure to incorporate as many of your senses as possible. What would you see if you had your outcome? What would you hear, feel, smell, taste and touch? Specificity is a must for measurable and predictable results.

The more specific and more complete your Outcome Frame is, the more effectively your unconscious mind will create the positive feelings you want and need. That begins to create the Deli Sign phenomenon.

— 49 —

Instead of seeing problems, you'll begin to see solutions. Instead of feeling miserable and stuck you'll feel focused, motivated and full of creative energy.

With the Outcome Frame your unconscious will automatically begin to fill in the gaps and help you see the Deli Signs along the way.

Turn to the page entitled, "Problem Frame vs. Outcome Frame". Write the answers to the questions and simply notice what you begin to experience. Notice what you are feeling in terms of the first set of questions and then in terms of the second set of questions. Do this before you go any farther.

What did you find out? One of the most curiously amazing things to me is how powerful Framing really is. Remember those negative feelings that you began to experience looking at the Problem Frame? Did you feel stimulated and motivated to act positively? No, of course not!

However, how did you feel when you reframed the problem into the Outcome Frame? Did you experience a sense of freedom, of power and a sense of possibility? The Outcome Frame is the think-feel-do-have success formula in action. The same powerful formula — What you think about, you begin to feel; and what you feel, you begin to do; and what you do, you begin to have.

Perhaps you can now begin to see how the Outcome Frame, or any frame, actually creates reality!

When you create and hold this Outcome Frame, you create power and action in three ways. One, you set up an aim, or trajectory, toward your goal. Two, you filter out unnecessary stimuli and distractions that may tend to get in your way or tend to get you off track. And three, by holding an Outcome Frame, you allow in only what is associated with the frame of mind that leads to achieving the desired outcome. Your unconscious mind fills in the gaps and you can see the Deli Signs!

Think back again to your problem point of view in the activity you just did. That's the Frame many hold so much of the time. It doesn't feel good, does it? You can really feel the limitations. It points to the negative. It leads to blaming others or blaming ourselves. I call it the *Blame Frame*. It creates and leads to symptoms of fear and stress. Finally, it can even lead to constriction, destruction and collapse.

Now remember your Outcome Frame again for a moment. Notice the difference in how you feel. The Outcome Frame feels good, positive and motivational. It is constructive and it leads you toward exciting possibilities.

The Outcome Frame creates more awareness, more flexibility of thought and action. It gives you more choices. It's expansive. In fact, the Outcome Frame, just the Outcome Frame alone, when appropriately utilized, can help you get and stay motivated. It can assist you in controlling your mind and your feelings, and in expanding your comfort zone. Perhaps you can see why the Outcome Frame is a major secret to unlocking the power of the think-feel-do-have motivation and success formula?

So, anytime you have a problem or something that makes you feel stuck or limited, reframe the problem. Use the Outcome Frame and transform that problem into a challenging opportunity. See and feel the difference this will make in your life. Each time you do you will be providing yourself with an incredible opportunity to exercise your creativity.

PROBLEM FRAME VS OUTCOME FRAME

Purpose: To experience how an Outcome Frame of mind can generate more freedom, power and choice in your life.

I. Write down something that is a Problem in your life right now.

_____

_____

PROBLEM FRAME

II. Write briefly your answers to the following questions relating to your problem.

1. What's wrong? _____

_____

2. Why do I have this problem? _____

_____

3. How does it limit me? _____

_____

4. What does this problem stop me from doing that I want to do? ___

_____

5. Whose fault is it that I have this problem? _____

_____

6. When is the worst time I have experienced this problem?

_____

_____

_____

7. How long have I had it? _____

(Now go to Outcome Frame)

OUTCOME FRAME

III. Now let's Do Something Different. Write brief answers to these questions relating to the same problem.

1. What do I want instead of the problem? _____

_____

2. When do I want it? _____

_____

3. How will I know that I have it? _____
   (What will I see, hear, feel when I have what I want?)

_____

_____

4. When I get what I want, what else in my life will improve?

_____

5. What resources do I have available to me to help me achieve this

   outcome? _____

_____

6. What resources do I need to attain my Outcome? _____

_____

7. What am I now going to do to get what I want? _____

_____

IV. Question to consider regarding activity:

1. How did I feel differently during the second set of questions as

   opposed to the first set? _____

_____

Note: You can photocopy Problem Frame vs. Outcome Frame for repeated use.

SUMMARY

This book is already teaching you to control the think-feel-do-have success formula — the process that creates the feeling, the actions, and the results you want to have in you life. In fact, controlling the think-feel-do-have success formula is exactly the same thing as having the three keys to personal power.

In the upcoming chapters we are going to explore the think-feel-do-have success formula more thoroughly and focus on the *feel* part specifically. This is because the *feel* part is really the pivotal point in controlling the think-feel-do-have formula more purposefully and easily. That's why the Keying process is so exciting.

After exploring the various steps of the techniques in controlling your feelings, we are going to put them all back together and then drop them into your unconscious mind so you can use them automatically and habitually.

By using what you have learned in an automatic way, you will have more personal power and get the things that you really want in life. Then in an emergency, when you need to consciously use the techniques you have learned, these methods will spring to your mind for overcoming your fears, satisfying your needs, or helping you with whatever challenging opportunity in which you find yourself.

When you have completed this exciting system, all the knowledge and processes in your book will have become a permanent powerful part of your life. You will truly be the master of your feelings and emotions and the master of your future.

You will find yourself feeling and thinking in new ways; ways that are more vigorous, more focused and more positive. You'll experience the feelings you want when you want them. You'll live free of fear, anxiety and self-doubts. You'll have created a clear and fulfilling plan for your future. A future you can create with feelings of confidence and satisfaction. And perhaps, and this is the most important thing of all, you'll be enjoying life more and more each day.

One last thought, it might be encouraging to know that you don't have to be perfect in every activity you learn in this book. You didn't learn to walk by walking, you learned to walk by falling down and then getting up. Simply allow yourself the freedom to have some fun in learning and doing the various activities suggested. The unconscious mind will fill in the gaps!

At first, some people think the methods are a little mechanical or too techniquish. However, after experiencing some of the profound effects, many come to realize the depth and pervasiveness of their change. Like I say in my seminars and cassette programs, "When in doubt, check it out."

You might also be interested to know that there is a process in neuro-linguistic programming™ called "generative change". What this means is one positively learned piece of behavior generates two additional positive chunks of behavior and consequently those two will generate four more — and on — and on.

So learning just one thing will make an impact in every area of your life. Imagine what you have already accomplished. Let's now move into deeper understanding of the think-feel-do-have success formula.

Because of the way *psychoneurolinguistics* works, your simply reading this far in your *Keying: The Power Of Positive Feelings*, changes in your world are already occurring in fascinating ways. Your new awareness and understanding of the integral connection between your body and your mind is allowing you to consciously make choices that will change your life to the more successful and more powerful life you've always wanted.

You can now think in terms of making the think-feel-do-have success formula begin to work for you. Perhaps you are allowing yourself to know that the "impossible" truly is possible.

You have begun to look at your Problem Frames and as you look, you've begun to reframe them into positive Outcome Frames.

Your body/mind set is focused on learning to control your feelings and your mind no matter what the circumstance. Exciting changes are in motion right now as you progress to the next chapter, "THE 'KEY': CONTROLLING YOUR FEELINGS, YOUR BEHAVIOR, AND YOUR LIFE."

Above all, have fun! And keep your eyes open for the Deli Signs along the way!

CHAPTER III.

THE "KEY": CONTROLLING YOUR FEELINGS, YOUR BEHAVIOR, AND YOUR LIFE

THIS IS IT!

In the previous sections you were introduced to the concept of body/mind and how your body and mind interconnect and support each other. You learned how to use the information to actively begin making the think-feel-do-have success formula work for you.

However, this is the section you've been waiting for. In this chapter you will begin to control the principle element to personal power: controlling your feelings. You will learn to control your feelings easily and quickly. One of the areas people have always wanted is the power to control their emotions.

From the *Hunas*, the oldest and most ancient religion of *positive thinking*, past the century old martial arts practices of the *Ninja's magic hand signals*, to the more recent approach of *Pavlov's stimulus/response conditioning*, Keying has been and can now be applied to all current strategies of successful living.

By using the power techniques in this section, you will never have to be the victim of your feelings ever again. This section deals with the *feel* part of the think-feel-do-have motivation and success formula.

In this section you will learn how to use Keying to control your feelings so you can feel what you want, when you want, no matter what you're thinking or what is going on around you.

With Keying you will learn how to wash away anxiety, fears and even major phobias.

By using your Key you will learn how to end procrastination and how to motivate yourself instantly.

You will learn specific ways to wash away negative and unwanted feelings associated with the past.

The Keying process can also be used to redirect and reshape your future predictably, successfully and in exciting ways, dissolving limiting blocks and barriers forever.

With the information in this section, you will begin to change your life in the ways you have always wanted. It is precisely the information that will allow you to achieve your dreams.

YOU NEVER HAVE TO HAVE ANOTHER BAD DAY!

Learning the Keying techniques will give you conscious control over your feelings, moods and emotions forever. When you can control how you feel, you can enjoy the rest of your life feeling great and living as well as you feel.

RANDOM "KEYS" —
YOU CANNOT *NOT* "KEY"

Were you ever in love, then after you broke up, you began to feel those certain sensations every time you drove by your former lover's house. Or every time you saw their car, or even a car like theirs, you began to feel that certain way?

Those are examples of Keys. Your former lover's house or car had become a stimulus, a Key that triggered an automatic feeling response in you.

Our daily lives are filled with Keys or stimuli that trigger responses in us. For example, do you have a favorite song and every time you hear that song or even think of that song, you get those certain feelings? Or maybe a favorite restaurant and every time you go to that restaurant or think of that restaurant you feel good?

Have you ever gotten a speeding ticket and every time you drive by the spot on the road where you got your speeding ticket, you slow down and look around and remember when you got that speeding ticket? All of those are examples of Keys.

A Key is any stimulus that triggers an automatic response.

Words and thoughts can be Keys also. For example, what do you feel when you think of the word "mother" Or how about the word "blue"? Depending upon the associations made with those words, you will have certain feelings. For example, with the word blue, a lot of people see water or the sky and they feel good. But other people think of Blue Monday or they think of times when they felt sad.

The people in our lives can also be Keys. Is there a person in your life who, if they walked through your door right now, you would smile and your heart would skip a beat and you would feel wonderful? That person is a positive Key in your life. They have become a stimulus that creates in you an automatic positive feeling response.

On the other hand, maybe you can think of a person who, if they walked through the door would make you cringe and think "Oh no!" That person has become a negative Key.

A person's voice can be a Key or even someone's tone of voice. I remember when I was a boy. If I heard my mother say "Donny," in a certain way I felt good. I knew that everything was okay. But sometimes when I heard her say, in a firmer voice, "Donald!" my body would automatically get tense. I knew that I was in trouble, so it would perhaps take me somewhat longer to get into the house.

A smell can be one of the strongest Keys known. Each one of us has our own pet positive and negative smells that create certain feelings in us.

Anything can become a Key: a voice, a smell, a touch, a person, a place, a song, a memory or a thought about the future. All of these things can trigger automatic feeling responses. We human beings are very programmable. We very easily make these automatic connections between Keys and the way we feel.

Many of our feelings, and our moods, from moment to moment are caused by Keys that often we are not even aware of. Keying is going on all the time in so many areas and most of the time randomly and unconsciously. In fact, YOU CANNOT *NOT* KEY!

PURPOSEFUL "KEYS"

The examples I have just given you are random Keys. They just happen because stimulus-response keying is a natural process. People can also use what I call purposeful Keys. Purposeful Keys are powerful Keys created on purpose to make us respond in certain ways.

Stop signs and red lights are examples of purposeful Keys. They have been developed purposefully to trigger us to respond in a certain way. We do not have to think, we just respond. A good example of this is when I found myself late one night in the country at a four way stop sign. Although I could see for miles in every direction, I still slowed down and stopped. That is what I had been Keyed to do.

Our flag is also a Key. When we look at the flag, we feel patriotic. When you hear music associated with the flag, like John Phillips Sousa's music or the national anthem, how do you feel? Hearing John Phillips Sousa's music, automatically, causes us to feel patriotic.

The sound of a siren Keys us into being alert or afraid and cautious. We don't think, we don't analyze. We hear a siren and automatically we feel alert.

Advertising is a great example of using purposeful Keys and the Keying process. Advertisers try to connect their products or services with experiences we value highly. They connect their products with feelings in us such as comfort, quality, pleasure, value and excitement.

What do you think of when you think about the word Volkswagen? Now think of the word Mercedes. Compare your two feelings. Volkswagen attempts to key their name with economy. Mercedes is keying their brand name with luxury and quality.

If their advertising works, the connection between the car names and your feelings is effective. Every time you hear that name or see that brand name you will feel the emotion they want you to feel and you are more apt to buy.

The perfume industry is an example where millions

of dollars are spent developing name and fragrance Keys that will elicit specific feelings.

Do you remember this saying, "Things go better with ----."? What did you fill in the gap with? Things go better with *Coke*. That slogan has not been said on radio or television, or been seen in print for over 25 years and you still remember! That is how powerful and how long a Key can last. Forever! And that's how transferable a Key can be. Some have never actually heard the commercial, yet knew the answer because they had heard it from others.

Let's review the important points of Keying, random and purposeful keys. One, a Key is a stimulus that creates an automatic feeling response in us. We don't have to even think about it, we simply respond. Two, anything can be a Key: a sound, a smell, a person, a voice, a memory, a thought, a place, a touch. Three, you cannot *not* Key. Keying is going on all the time, mostly unconsciously.

If you do not learn to control the Keying process, the Keying process will control you. You will find yourself living a life where your emotions, your feelings and your actions are the result of unconscious, haphazard Keys and you end up producing haphazard results in your life.

On the other hand, as you learn to consciously control the Keying process, you can begin to control your moods and your feelings and then, you can begin to control your actions. You then can have control over the results and achievements in your life.

The goal is to learn how to have more personal power that will produce the results you want. In order to do that, you need to become more aware of the various Keys that are around you and the feelings they trigger.

Then if a certain Key is not helping you attain your

goals, or if a certain Key is causing you to feel some way you don't like, with your Keying process you can quickly create a positive new Key to replace that negative Key. A powerful and positive Key which will create the feelings you want and need.

Like I have said so many times, when you learn the techniques in this book you will never have to have another bad day. You will have the power to consciously create the feelings you want. You can consciously create the moods you want.

You will be creating several powerful Keys which you can use at any time. You will be creating a confidence Key, a motivation Key so you can be motivated any time you want, a relaxation Key so you can create feelings of ease and relaxation whenever you want.

You can create a decision-making Key, one that you can use in those times when you are stuck or indecisive and don't quite know what to do.

And you will create a curiosity and wonder Key so that each time you use it you will respond with feelings of curiosity and wonder — like a child who sees each moment and each day as a fresh new beginning. The feelings of joy and amazement you felt when you were a child.

HISTORY OF "KEYING"

Let's talk about the history of Keying and how I "discovered" it.

Keying is a natural and automatic process but, not until recently has the Keying process itself been isolated so it can be taught in such a way that it can change your life easily and simply.

Does the name *Pavlov* ring a bell? I'm sure you remember what Pavlov did in his classic reflex conditioning experiments.

Pavlov put meat in front of a hungry dog. As the dog salivated, Pavlov would ring a bell. Then he did it again. He put meat in front of the dog, the dog salivated and at the same time he rang the bell. Pavlov put the meat in front of the dog and rang the bell only four times — *only four times!* Then he threw the meat away and when he would ring the bell the dog automatically salivated with no meat.

After only four pairings of the salivation and the ringing of the bell, the salivation and the ringing of the bell became linked together, or connected, in the dog's brain and body. After only four trials.

It is important to note, the dog then spontaneously salivated with no New Year's resolutions, no burning desires, no psychoanalysis, no psychotherapy, no subliminal tapes, no will power or no positive thinking or affirmations. It was straight neurological conditioning. That's what Keying is: straight body memory conditioning.

When I was doing research for the National Institute of Mental Health at the Veteran's Administration Hospital, a report crossed my desk telling about soldiers who were wounded and sent to the hospital. They were treated for their wounds and administered morphine for the pain. The wounds healed but the soldiers became morphine addicts.

Some very curious researchers thought, "Why don't we do with the patients what Pavlov did with the dog?" However, instead of ringing a bell, these researchers would rub the patient's forearm and at the same time they would inject the morphine. Rubbing the forearm was the bell, that was the Key. They would rub the patient's forearm and at the same time they would inject

WHAT "KEYING" IS NOT

- Positive Thinking
- Willpower
- Positive Mental Attitude
- Belief
- Visualization
- Affirmations
- Wishful Thinking
- Spaced Repetition
- New Year's Resolutions
- Related to Self-Esteem
- Logic or Reason
- Self-Hypnosis
- Motivational Self-Talk
- Subliminal Programming
- Psychotherapy
- Complicated

WHAT KEYING IS

- ☐ Stimulus-response
- ☐ Straight neurological programming
- ☐ Simple
- ☐ Measurable
- ☐ Predictable
- ☐ Lasting

the morphine. Now they only did that four or five times and then they started reducing the amount of morphine.

Eventually, they threw the needle away and when the patients needed morphine, they would simply rub the patient's forearm and the patient's body would remember enough of the pain killing experience that the soldiers were cured of their addiction.

They had no withdrawal symptoms that normally accompany morphine withdrawal. They had no aggravation, no irritability or depression.

The soldiers, like Pavlov's dog, used no New Year's resolutions, no will power, no positive thinking, no visualization or psychotherapy. Keying is not any of those things. It is straight neurological conditioning. It is simple, predictable, measurable and lasting.

Keying bypasses the thinking process completely. Keying is pure physiological conditioning. Pure, neurological programming of body memories. That's why it works so powerfully and so fast.

The results of this research made me curious and I began thinking, "My goodness, if that kind of conditioning is strong enough to use against a powerful physical addiction such as morphine, what would happen if it were used with fear addicts or negative thinking addicts or poverty addicts?"

What I did not know, however, was how to get people to feel the feeling they needed or desired in the first place. That was the question. I knew morphine wasn't the answer. How could a person first create the feeling they wanted so they could Key it in? That is, how could they make the connection and lock in the feelings with the Keying process?

I started doing research training in what's called neuro-linguistic programming™ with John Grinder, one of the founders. I would like to note that some of the words used in this book are words of art and came from John Grinder and neuro-linguistic programming™.

I also studied the works of the late medical hypnotist, Milton H. Erickson. One of the things Dr. Erickson said was so simple it was profound. It was exactly what I was looking for. It was the missing link and I've mentioned it many times already. He said, "What you think about, you begin to feel."

If you think about somebody you like, you feel good. If you think about somebody you don't like, you feel bad. It's so simple and yet so powerful.

I also recalled a study in the "secrets" of the Ninja, an obscure martial arts form. The Ninjas used physical reminders to reinforce certain feelings when conquering fear before going into battle.

Centuries ago the physical reminder was called a *"magic hand signal."* More recently Pavlov called it *classical conditioning.* Neuro-linguistics call it *anchoring.* I call it *Keying.* It doesn't matter what you call it, as long as it creates an instantaneous replay of any feelings you want.

PUTTING IT ALL TOGETHER

Now let's put it all together. What you think about, you begin to feel, and what you feel, you can Key in. And then every time you use the Key, you can get an instant replay of that chosen feeling again and again.

Keying is so exciting because it's a major breakthrough in behavioral change. Keying is the next step beyond positive thinking. It is the next step beyond self hypnosis, beyond affirmations and visualizations and beyond psychotherapy.

Keying does much more than positive thinking or holding a positive mental attitude because with Keying you learn to create and control your positive *feelings*. And what you *feel* you begin to *do*. And Keying works fast, it is measurable and it is predictable.

With Keying you'll be able to break the fear chain and feel calm and relaxed, even if you're thinking fearful and negative thoughts. With Keying you'll learn to create positive feelings at will and greatly expand your comfort zone so that you can have more money, deeper relationships, more joy and excitement. You'll never have to fall back into old unsuccessful feelings and behaviors again. With Keying you will be able to take advantage of the mysterious and "magical" Deli Sign phenomenon.

EXAMPLES OF "KEYS" AND THE "KEYING" PROCESS

Once I realized that what we think about we begin to feel, and what we begin to feel we can Key in. I then knew I had all the pieces to the puzzle. I started experimenting at the Phobia Institute of West Los Angeles in California.

Arnold, a young a stockbroker, came into my office having a terrible time. After getting a lot of "no's" and being rejected very often when talking to prospective clients on the telephone, Arnold began to be fearful and shy about even making telephone calls.

The telephone had become a negative Key for him. He started backing away from the telephone because it triggered off horrible feelings of rejection when he heard people say "no."

Eventually, he would not even go to his office because the whole office had generalized into and had become a negative Key. He would wake up in the morning and he would just think about his office and feel horrible. His career was at a standstill.

So I asked him, "Arnold, when you pick up the telephone and talk, how would you like to feel instead?" He said, "I would like to feel confident again. I would like to feel sure of myself and feel excited."

So I asked him, "Arnold, have you ever felt excited and motivated before?" He said "Sure." I had him remember a time when he felt really excited. And when I could see he was really feeling excited from thinking of that memory, I had him pick up the telephone.

Then I had him remember another time when he felt really excited, really interested and motivated, raring to go for it. When I could see he was really feeling good from remembering that time, I had him pick up the telephone again.

We repeated this just a few more times and then I said, "Arnold, let's test our work. Do not remember any time you were excited and just pick up the phone and see how you feel." He picked up the phone and after three or four seconds he began to feel excited.

The phone had been changed to a positive Key! Well, he couldn't believe it. I even had difficulty in believing it. He was amazed that the Keying process was so fast and so powerful.

He was able then not only to go back to his office, but he was also able to be there feeling very comfortable and very excited and motivated.

The phone has now become a permanent positive Key for him. He now picks up the phone and looks forward to talking to people feeling very excited. Feelings he needed to be successful. What he had done was not only wash away the negative telephone Key, but he also made the telephone a positive Key.

Mary, a young woman came into my office one day. She had been married for only a few years and she told me she wanted to get a divorce. This story is so interesting because it really demonstrates how powerfully negative Keys can limit our lives and how quickly and powerfully developing a positive Key can change our lives.

I asked, "Mary, why do you want to get a divorce?" And she said, "It's because I have fallen out of love." Now, that has always intrigued me, people falling in and falling out of love. So I asked her, "How do you know you have fallen out of love?" And she said, "Every time my husband touches me I feel bad. Therefore, I don't love him. Therefore, I want to get a divorce."

After asking her a few more questions, I found out that she had been depressed off and on over the past year or two. When her husband, a very loving and caring man, would come home from work and she would be depressed and feeling bad, he would reach out and put his arm around her and say, "Don't feel depressed Mary." Remember "Don'ts" don't work. Actually, they do work, only backwards. They can create an opposite reaction.

In this case Mary was getting a double whammy. His saying "Don't" *and* his touching her became a negative Key! So, every time he would put his arm around her, it triggered those depressed feelings and she would feel bad. Her feeling bad became an automatic response and therefore she thought that she did not love him anymore. Therefore, she wanted to get a divorce.

When I found that out I asked, "Mary, how would you like to feel good when your husband hugged you, whether you left him or not?" Well, she thought that was a pretty good idea and one she could not refuse.

So I asked her husband to come in with her the following week. I then had her remember times she was feeling full of love and cared for. Then, when she was feeling those good feelings very, very strongly, I had her husband walk over and put his arm around her *while she was feeling good.*

He only had to do that four or five times. Then instead of a negative Key he became a positive Key and every time he would put his arm around her she would feel good, rather than bad.

That Key was a permanent positive Key because she and her husband are still living happily together. She realized they had quite a lot in common and they are happily married even to this day.

Here's another example of Keying. A little 13 year old boy, Billy, was afraid and fearful because he had to give a talk in front of his class the next day. I had him remember times when he felt calm and relaxed, having some fun. As he did that he began feeling relaxed. I then had Billy rub his forearm like the soldier at the Veterans Administration Hospital. He did that two or three times. Then, the next day he rubbed his forearm just before giving his talk and his body automatically became relaxed and he did quite well. And he said he even had fun doing it!

Since developing the Keying process, I have been able to teach it to thousands of people throughout the world, people who have changed their lives for the better. And I am so happy to be able to share this knowledge with you now.

TRY IT YOURSELF!

This is about the time people start to get a little overwhelmed and doubtful. They just cannot believe the Keying process is so simple and so powerful. So let's do a Keying experiment right now.

All of the activities are presented like the ones in the cassette program "Through The Briar Patch" that has help thousands to better their lives. As you read,

I'll be guiding you along. You can do them as you read or put the book down. It doesn't matter.

I am going to have you squeeze your left knee and then you will squeeze your right knee. The squeezing of your knees will be your Keys for now. Do the activity first. Then I'll explain what happened later.

So the first thing I would like you to do is think of somebody you like. I mean think of somebody you really like who makes you feel really good. Someone when you think of them, you begin to feel those good feelings inside your body. Yea, that's the one. Now gently reach down and squeeze your left knee.

Now think of that same person you really like again or think of somebody else that you really like who gives you those good feelings. Think again of somebody who gives you good feelings inside your body and as you feel those pleasant feelings, gently reach down and, again in the same way, squeeze your left knee. Do it in the same place and with the same pressure.

Let's do it one more time. Think of that someone you really, *really* like. Imagine them being really close to you and be with them, create that person bigger than life in your mind. When you get those good feelings, reach down, gently squeeze your left knee and on the same place and with the same pressure.

Now, let's sort of come back to a neutral or natural feeling state. Kind of jiggle your body around, focus outside and think of something else. Something neutral.

What I would like you to do now is think of someone or some situation you don't like or that mildly disgusts you. Just one. One that makes you feel uncomfortable or disgusted. You know the one. That's the one. Okay.

When you start feeling those disgusting negative feelings, just a little bit, gently reach down and squeeze your right knee.

Alright, let's do it again. One more time. I won't have you feel those bad feelings very long. Remember that person, again, or that situation you don't like or disgusts you and when you get those feelings of disgust, just gently reach down on your right knee and squeeze the same place with the same gentle pressure. Good.

Let's again get into our neutral state. Think of something else. Focus outside or move your body around a little.

Now from your *neutral state,* let's *test* your Keys and notice what happens. Gently reach down and on the same place and with the same pressure, just squeeze your left knee. Give it a little squeeze and notice what you begin to think and begin to feel. Give it a few seconds. Notice what you begin to think and feel.

Now go to a neutral state. Alright, let's go to the right knee. Now gently squeeze your right knee exactly the way you did before and notice what begins to happen, what you begin to think and what you begin to feel.

Go to your neutral state for a moment. Now just reach out, and gently squeeze your left knee again. Notice what begins to happen and how you begin to feel differently!

Amazing isn't it!

Let's do an even more exciting experiment. Gently hold the positive Key (your left knee) — and then think those negative thoughts. Notice, what you're doing is thinking negative and feeling positive! You have put a *wedge* in between your negative thinking and your positive feeling!

Now, that's how fast Keying works! It's quick because Keying is straight neurological commands.

YOU DON'T HAVE TO BELIEVE IT

With the Keying process, you can create the feelings you want when you want without will power, without New Year's Resolutions. You don't have to believe it to have it work. It works without positive thinking, and without subliminal tapes. By simply using the Keying process itself, you can control your body memories and your feelings.

Now in this experiment you created very strong Keys, or maybe you created less intense positive and negative Keys. It really doesn't matter because what you are learning is how to use this Keying process consciously so you can create the feelings you want and have more control over your feelings. The more you practice the Keying process, the stronger your Keys will be and the more effective they will be.

CREATING A "KEY" WITH THE POWER OF POSITIVE FEELINGS

THE STEPS IN "KEYING"

Now, let's go through the steps in Keying in detail so you will be able to recreate any kind of feelings you would like to have, any time you want, for the rest of your life. The steps in Keying are very simple.

STEP ONE in Keying is to determine what your Key will be. In the activity we just did, we determined that the Key would be squeezing the left knee for a positive Key. That was a good effective Key because it was unique, unusual. You don't usually go around squeezing your left knee when you want to feel good.

It had the three characteristics of a good Key. You used the *proper timing*. You squeezed the knee exactly when you felt those good feelings, the ones you wanted to feel strongly and fully. You squeezed your knee exactly the same way each time, with the *same pressure*, in the *same location*, and for the same length of time. The characteristics of a good Key are same place, same timing, same pressure.

STEP TWO in Keying is to acknowledge your current feelings, and give thanks for them. You'll understand why as you continue through the book. For now, just recognize, acknowledge and accept the way you are feeling before you go on.

STEP THREE. Decide what you want to feel instead, then create those feelings. Ask yourself, "What do I want to feel instead?" In the activity we did, I wanted you to feel good. That was the desired feeling state. Then, I asked you to create that desired state of feeling good by thinking of people who made you feel really good. The mind and the body never forget unless there is some intervention made.

STEP FOUR. When you feel the positive feelings intensely and fully, Key them in. That is, pair them up with your Key. In the experiment, you squeeze that knee every time you felt those good feelings strongly.

STEP FIVE is to *stack* the Key. Stacking the Key is simply repeating the Keying process. That is, think again of a person who makes you feel good or times when you felt the way you want to feel and Key that in. Then, think of other people or other times that make you feel the way you want and when you feel those feelings strongly, Key them in.

STEPS IN "KEYING"

KEY: The Key is a predetermined stimulus that lets your body record and re-experience any feeling you want.

KEYING: A way to "lock in" and "unlock" any feelings you want regardless of what you are thinking or what is going on around you. It can also be used to wash away negative feelings associated with past trauma as well as to program new behavior for the future.

Steps in Keying

1. Determine what your Key will be.

2. Acknowledge your current feelings.

3. Decide what you want to feel instead and create that Desired State.*

    (a) Ask yourself, "Have I ever had a time when I felt the way I want to feel?" Then, remember that time. (The mind and body never forget.)
    (b) Remember other times you felt the way you want to feel.
    (c) Act "As If" you felt the way you want to feel.

4. Key in those feelings when the desired state is fully felt. (Pair up your Key with the desired feeling.)

5. Stack the Key by feeling your desired state several times and Keying it in each time with the same Key.

6. Get into your Neutral state.

7. Test the Key by firing it off. If the test produces the desired feelings, go on to the next step. If not, stack the Key some more or repeat the entire process.

8. Applications of the Key.

    (a) Using in Current Situations
    (b) Letting go of the Past
    (c) Re-directing the Future

See page "Creating a Strong Desired State" for additional ways of producing the feelings you want.

CHARACTERISTICS OF A GOOD KEY

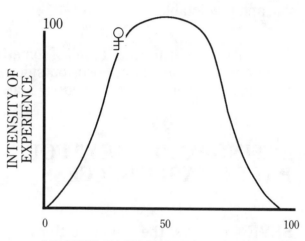

LENGTH OF TIME OF EXPERIENCE

NOTE: For optimum results, just before the experience peaks (at the sign of the ♀), fire off or insert your predetermined Key. You can squeeze your wrist, wiggle your big toe, or whatever you've decided is the best Key for you.

THE THREE CHARACTERISTICS OF A GOOD KEY

1. Use the same exact location.

2. Use the same exact pressure or intensity.

3. Use the same exact timing. Fire off the Key just before the desired feelings peak each time.

So to stack the Key, you feel your desired feeling several times and each time when the feeling is strong, Key it in. Stacking adds several good feelings to the same Key. And so the Key becomes much stronger and more reliable and predictable.

STEP SIX is go to a neutral state. Think of something else. Get up and move around a bit. Focus outside yourself. Do anything to get yourself into a neutral state.

TESTING YOUR "KEY" FOR PREDICTABLE SUCCESS

STEP SEVEN is to *test* the Key. One thing I pride myself about is everything you'll learn with psychoneurolinguistics can be testable and predictable. Our motto at the Phobia Institute is, "If you can't test it, don't do it!"

To test your Key start in a neutral state. You're feeling what you normally feel in your neutral state. Then fire off your Key and within two to seven seconds you will begin to feel those positive feelings you previously Keyed in. If, within two to seven seconds, those feelings come back very strongly, then you have a good strong Key.

If the feelings are not as strong as you would like, then go back and stack the Key some more. Create the feelings of your desired state again and Key them in. Keep repeating the process until, when you test the Key, you have good strong physical recall and an instant replay of those desired feelings. The test I like best is to fire off the stacked Key and when you get those desire feelings strongly, try to feel bad. If you can't, then you definitely have a good Key!

STEP EIGHT brings us to applications. You're ready to use your Key in current, past and future situations. You are now ready for the various applications and you'll be learning all of these shortly.

CHARACTERISTICS OF A GOOD "KEY"

But, first, let's review the characteristics of a good Key. You may want to refer to the page entitled "Characteristics of a Good Key".

Remember, to get a good strong Key choose something that is unique. Something that you would not use or do accidentally. It can be squeezing your knee, like we used in our activity, or maybe, squeezing your wrist or pushing your thumb and index finger together, or wiggling your big toe if you don't want to be obvious. It doesn't matter whatever you decide.

Then, keep in mind when you fire off the Key, you want to do it the same way each time and do it in the same place, with the same pressure and for the same length of time.

Also, You'll want to fire off your Key just as those desired feelings are peaking, when you begin to feel them very, very strongly and fully. Fire off the Key when the feelings you want are very strong and yet could still get a little bit stronger.

SEVEN STEPS TO A STRONGER "KEY"

What are some ways to create a strong, powerful desired state? The stronger your desired feelings are, the stronger your Key will be. See the page entitled "Creating a Strong Effective Key or Desired State".

To create a strong and powerfully effective Key, you obviously want to create strong and intense feelings to Key in. How do you create the stronger feelings so you can Key them in?

One of the best ways to get the feelings you want more intense is to Key in the desired feelings when you are actually doing something that gives you those feelings.

For example, let's say you are building a confidence Key, which we will be doing shortly. Let"s say, you have decided that your Key is to squeeze your left wrist. Then, every time you find yourself doing things with confidence and feeling confident, take the opportunity then to squeeze your left wrist and Key in those confident feelings.

If on Monday morning you make a big sale or you do something, anything that makes you feel confident and assured, take the opportunity to squeeze your left wrist and Key in those feelings. Let's say later in the day you do something else that makes you feel confident, gently squeeze your wrist again and add those confident feelings to your Key.

The second way to create a strong and powerful Desired State is to remember a time in the past when you had the feelings you want — a time when you felt really confident. As you remember that time and you begin to feel those strong feelings, again Key them in using the same Key.

The third way to create strong desired feelings is to remember many different times when you had the feelings you want to have now. You can remember numerous times when you felt confident and assured. As you remember those times and the feelings get fuller and stronger, gently squeeze your wrist. Using the same Key, at the same time, with the same pressure and Key them in.

CREATING A STRONG DESIRED STATE

1. As you are doing an activity that creates feelings you want, Key them in.

2. Remember a time when you had the state you want now.

3. Remember different times you felt the way you want to feel.

4. Act "As If" you felt the way you want. What would you be doing if you were in your desired state?

   a. Stand the way you would stand.

   b. Make the facial expression you would have.

   c. Say what you would say the way you would say in if you felt the way you want.

   The more completely you act "As If" the more powerfully you will create your desired state.

5. Be in the Associated State. Jump inside your mental pictures and mentally be there.

6. Think of a person you admire and respect doing and having the feelings and state you want. Then go into Associated State.

7. Listen to appropriate music, radio shows; watch your favorite television shows, movies, sunsets: or say your choice affirmation or prayer.

8. Repeat the Keying Process as often as needed.

A fourth way is to act "As If". I call this the "As If" Frame. Ask yourself the question, "What would I be doing, how would I be acting and feeling if I had the confident feelings I want?"

Now I mean that literally. Ask yourself, "What posture would I have?" Get into that posture. "How would I stand? What facial expression would I have? What kind of tone and tempo would my voice have?" Involve and engage yourself in it completely. Begin to act "As If" you have those feelings. Your unconscious mind can't tell the difference between a vividly imagined and felt state and a real one. As you begin to get those positive, confident feelings, Key them in.

A fifth way is to be in the *associated state*. Now what does that mean? Often when you are remembering something, it is "as if" you are sitting in the audience of a movie theatre watching yourself on the screen. You're disassociated from — not involved with the scene.

If you associate into the screen, however, that is, you think of yourself actually entering into the "movie" as if you were there, you will find that the associated feelings will become stronger. You will feel more involved and more engaged. Then you can Key in those feelings.

A sixth way to create strong desired feelings is to think of a person you admire and respect. Then, imagine that person doing what you want to do and having the kind of feelings you want to have.

You might imagine someone you really look up to and you would see that person being confident, feeling confident and acting in a confident way. Then become that person in your imagination. That is, associate into that person's body. See the world as you think they see the world, feeling confident. Acting the way you think they act. This will create strong, confident feelings in you and then you can Key them in.

A seventh way to increase those desired feelings is to listen to appropriate music or listen to tapes. What kind of music makes you feel confident? What kind of movies? What kind of activities make you feel confident? Perhaps you have a favorite visualization, affirmation or prayer that gives you those good feelings. Do those things and, when you get the feelings, Key them in.

You can use all of the above methods or you can use one or two of them. But, remember to stack your key. Keep adding the same or similar feelings to your Key, over and over again, until it is as good and as strong and as effective as you want it to be.

CREATING A NEUTRAL STATE OR BAIL OUT "KEY'

Now, let's create a *neutral state* or a *bail out* Key. This is important because it can get you out of negative feelings or thoughts quickly. It also valuable by allowing you to effectively test your results and therefore, to determine what your next step will be. We'll go deeper into that later.

With future processes, you may choose to use this if you are starting to feel bad. Or you can use this bail out Key if you've been pulled back into the negative pictures, or you become overwhlemed by the negative self-talk in your mind and begin feeling the negative feeling and you need a way to get out quickly.

Also, you can use the bail out Key when you are stacking a Key or when you are getting ready to test your Key. You will want to be able to get into a neutral state first.

Now, what to do. Anything you do to break your concentration and change your feelings will quickly bring you into a neutral state. For example, changing your posture or getting up and moving around the room.

CREATING A NEUTRAL STATE
(The Bail Out Procedure)

PURPOSE: To get into a Neutral State and focus outside yourself.

1. Change what you are doing

2. Focus outside your mind into here and now

3. Change your position in room

4. Think of something else

5. Use diaphragmatic breathing

6. Establish a calm, relaxed, and alert Key prior to any activity

---

Opening your eyes and focusing outside yourself. You might look at something on the wall or look out the window.

A lot of people like to use diaphragmatic breathing. That is, deep belly breathing which slows down the heart rate, lowers blood pressure automatically and gets you into a calm and neutral state.

Another excellent way to create a neutral or bail out state is to create a relaxation bail out Key before you begin any activity. That way if you begin to feel more negative feelings than you would like, all you have to do is fire off your relaxation bail out Key and you will immediately go into a relaxed and neutral state.

Now you have all of the components to Keying. Perhaps you are curious to learn the various ways to apply it. In the following sections you will do just that. In the next chapter, to your amazement and surprise, with Keying you will not only learn how to increase your confidence and faith, but how to use Keying to increase all six Keys to complete personal power. Remember, personal power is getting what you want more often than not.

The six Keys to personal power are Confidence, Motivation, Creativity, Decisiveness, Relaxation, and Curiosity and Wonder. With these six Keys the world becomes the playground for all of the fun activities I believe it was intended to be.

CHAPTER IV.

CREATING THE "KEY" FOR FAITH AND CONFIDENCE

Let's create your own confidence Key. With that, you will be able to feel more confident and more assured any time you want. With the confidence Key, you can have more faith in your life.

IT'S IMPOSSIBLE TO FAIL!

As you begin to build your confidence Key, I want to give you some confidence by reminding you that it is impossible to fail. You can only succeed. Remember, in keying, as in all of the techniques you'll be learning, failure is impossible. You can get only results.

Keying is a natural process that has been working in your life ever since you were born. Perhaps you would like to look at it this way. With every result you get, think of it as the feedback you need that tells you what your next step is to be. Any time you create a Key, and the result is not as strong as you want it to be, that's telling you something very valuable.

The result is telling you what your next step could be. You may need to stack the Key. You may need to repeat the Keying process with the same feeling again using the same Key until the Key is as good and as strong as you'd like.

Perhaps what may seem astounding but yet true is, because you are doing these activities, you will find as you are sleeping and doing other things, even more resources and more confidence and more assurance is becoming part of your life. The unconscious mind is filling in the gaps.

STEPS IN CREATING A CONFIDENCE "KEY"

Now, you are going to create your own confidence Key. I will guide you as I would on my cassette programs or as if you were in my office. You can do the activity as you read if you like.

First, choose a Key. When you are using the Keying process by yourself, you can choose, of course, any Key that you want. But right now, for this activity, let's use squeezing your left wrist as the Key. It is unique. It is not something that you go around doing accidentally.

Each time you feel those feelings of confidence, you can reach over and gently squeeze your left wrist, using the same location, the same pressure and for the same length of time.

Next, acknowledge and give thanks for what you are feeling right now. Just notice and acknowledge the way you are feeling.

Then you want to decide what you want to feel instead. That is your desired state. It's the state that you are going to be Keying in. That state is confidence. You have already decided that you want to feel more confident and full of resources.

Now, let's go through some additional activities to get those confident feelings so you can Key them in. I will guide you as you answer the questions for yourself.

Have you ever felt confident before? Even if it were only for a moment, remember that time when you felt confident — when you were "going for it" and you were certain and sure of yourself. You were happy, you knew what you were doing. Now, as you remember that time, get those feelings, and when you can feel those feelings of confidence and self-assuredness fully, gently reach over and squeeze your left wrist.

Think of that time again. Remember that confident time again. As you feel the confident feelings fully now, reach over and gently squeeze your wrist once more. What you are doing is stacking the Key.

Now, remember another time when you felt confident, when you were focused outside, when you were centered and when you felt very self-assured. As you get those feelings very strongly, and you feel them just peaking all through your body, reach over and gently squeeze your left wrist and Key those confident feelings in. Use the same pressure, the same location and the same timing.

If you can, I suggest you stand up, walk around and act "as if" you have the faith you want. Act "as if" you are very confident, very self-assured. Change your posture. How would you be standing if you were extremely confident? What would your voice sound like? This acting "as if" creates even stronger body memories.

Move around like you would move around if you were confident. As you get those feelings of confidence coming into your body, reach over to your left wrist and Key them in. Remember, you can stack this Key with as many confident feelings as you want. With each stacking, you make it stronger. Remember another time when you were very, very confident and you were self-assured

— 88 —

and you felt good and were focused. Keep moving around. Let your body act in a confident way. As you get those feelings, gently reach over and Key them in.

Now, pretend you are seeing yourself as if you are in the audience of a movie theatre watching yourself being confident feeling very confident and self-assured on the screen. Then jump into the movie as if you were there. This will make the feelings even stronger. Now feel those feelings. Reach over and Key them in.

Can you think what it would be like if you were as self-assured as you'd like? If you felt very confident? Now, again, stand the way you would stand. Let your voice sound the way it would sound. Create how you would feel. Create how you would feel focused outside and feeling very, very confident. Feel those feelings of confidence. Reach over and gently squeeze your wrist and Key those feelings in. Great.

Now, go to your neutral state. Just focus outside of yourself for a moment, move around a little bit. Think of something else for a short period.

Let's now test your results from your neutral state. It is vital to measure your progress by testing each Key to see if it is strong enough. Gently reach over and squeeze your wrist. Fire off your Key in just the same way you have been doing and notice what happens. Allow two to seven seconds for those feelings of confidence to begin to return.

Don't expect a great big jolt that will knock you down. What you are looking for is to gradually feel the confident, assured feelings. If the feelings aren't quite as strong as you want them to be, that is, if you don't quite have the fully confident, assured feelings you would like, you can go back and stack the Key. That is, just repeat the process remembering other times you felt more confident, or acting "as if" you felt more confident, and then Key those feelings in.

Let's do that. Let's stack one more confident feeling on that Key. Think of somebody you really admire, someone you really respect. Someone who has the confidence and the self-assuredness you would like to have more of. Picture them now in your mind, having those confident feelings. See them acting in a confident, self-assured way, the way you would like to feel. Now, as you watch them doing the things you would like to do, imagine yourself stepping into their body, associate with their body, and see the world from their point of view and through their eyes. Notice how your feelings change.

As you feel more engaged and you begin feeling more self-assured and more confident, your posture will begin to change and your feelings inside will begin to feel more confident and more self-assured. As those feelings peak, reach over again, squeeze your wrist, and fire off that Key.

You can make your confidence Key even more powerful by repeating the Keying process you just went through and by using the methods for creating a stronger desired state as discussed earlier.

DEEPENING YOUR FAITH AND CONFIDENCE

Please turn to the page called "Generalizing and Future Programming". This written activity is to Future Pace the techniques and deepen the understandings that you have learned.

They will then be more deeply programmed into your unconscious and be more automatically available to you in the future.

I have found it extremely helpful to complete this activity as soon as you have finished with any of the other activities or any new learnings.

With the information that you've just read or with the activities you've just completed and with the new resources you've just acquired, you will list three occasions in the past in which the learnings and understanding would have been valuable to you.

After you have listed the past occasions, you will remember these situations, one at a time and starting with the most recent situation. Then, you will write a brief scenario as if you had had the new resources you've just learned, and as if you were there. Describe what you would have seen, heard, felt, smelled, tasted, using the new learnings now. Start at the beginning of the scenes and go a little beyond the end.

After that, you will think of the three situations in the future where these new techniques, learnings and understandings will be of value to you. Make the first in the near future, within a day or so. The second, later in time, a week to a month in the future. The third, the farthest from now — perhaps six, nine or twelve months from now. After you have written those, think of those situations one at a time.

Start with number one and write down what you would see, hear, feel, smell and taste, emotionally feel and do, "as if" you were already there now. Start at the beginning and go beyond the end of each scene. Seeing yourself in the future, using those new techniques, feeling and acting in the positive, powerful ways you want.

This important activity will program your brain and body to make these resources available to you whenever and wherever you need and want them. Again, I suggest you do this at the end of every activity.

Now as you let your unconscious fill in the gaps, let's look at some more curiously valuable resources you can learn to Key in and which you may find useful.

GENERALIZING AND FUTURE PROGRAMMING

Purpose: This activity is to actually program your brain and body with the new skills and information you've learned so that they deepen unconsciously and become an automatic part of your future.

A. With the information you've just read or listened to, with the activities you've just completed and with the new resources you've just acquired . . .

1. List three occasions in the PAST where the learnings and understandings would have been valuable to you.

a. _____

b. _____

c. _____

2. Now remember these situations, one at a time. Starting with the most recent, write the scenario "as if" you had had these new resources, and "as if" you are there. Describe what you would have seen, heard, felt, smelled, tasted, using the new learnings now. Start at beginning of the scenes and go a little beyond the end.

1. _____

_____

_____

2. _____

_____

_____

3. _____

_____

_____

B.

1. Now think of three situations in the FUTURE where these new learnings and understandings will be of value in adding choices to your behavior. Make the first in the near future, the second later in time and the third the farthest from now . . .

   a. _____

   _____

   b. _____

   _____

   c. _____

   _____

2. Now think of these situations one at a time. Start with number one and write down what you would see, hear, feel, smell and taste, emotionally feel and do, "as if" you were already there now. Start at the beginning and go beyond the end of each scene.

   1. _____

   _____

   2. _____

   _____

   3. _____

   _____

   _____

These are all positive resources for which you can create Keys to increase personal power. At first, for each of these positive resources states you'll want to use a different physical Key. Your confidence Key is squeezing your left wrist. For the other positive resource states, you may want to use something else. It might be wiggling your toes, or gently pinching your thunb and little finger together. Each different feeeling that you are Keying is to have a separate physical key and later on you can be more creative.

OTHER RESOURCE "KEYS" FOR PERSONAL POWER

It is exciting to know that you can take your confidence Key with you and use it in any situation and with any experience.

However, there are other positive resource states I would like to suggest. These states can be Keyed in and used in order to give you more control and more personal power. As I mentioned before, these five Keys, along with the confidence Key, have been found to be the six Keys to complete personal power.

MOTIVATION

The first additional resource Key is motivation. There are times when you get stuck, when you procrastinate. You don't have the motivating feelings you would like. Go back through the steps of the Keying process and create a strong *motivation Key* that can turn you on and get you excited any time you need it. Remember times when you were motivated and Key it in. Be sure to stack it and test it. Then, complete the generalizing and future programming activity. Motivation is now yours.

SIX "KEYS" TO PERSONAL POWER

(Use Separate Keys)

1. CONFIDENT/RESOURCEFUL: alert, aware, focused outside; forward and aggressive (without being pushy, angry or hostile).

2. MOTIVATION:

3. CREATIVITY:

   "stuck" → → → creative

4. DECISIVENESS:

5. RELAXATION:

   (a) Calm, relaxed, alert

   (b) Key it in for a 5 minute relaxation break

6. CURIOSITY AND FULL OF WONDER: Back to the childlike state. Wow! In awe!

CREATIVITY

Another valuable resource Key is the *creativity Key*. Maybe you're stuck in a project or a difficult situation or your creative juices just won't flow. Simply remember those times when you've felt extremely creative, or perhaps you can imagine what it would be like to be extremely creative. Key those feelings in. Stack and strengthen that Key. Now, you can carry instant creativity with you wherever you go.

DECISIVENESS

Wouldn't it be wonderful to create a *decisiveness Key* as a positive resource? Each of us faces situations where we just don't know what to do or we aren't sure of ourselves.

Where we're too afraid and we postpone making a decision, or maybe we never make a decision at all. Decisiveness, here, is yet another valuable resource Key. You can remember times that you were decisive and certain. Key those feelings in. You have now built a strong decisiveness Key which you can use in all of those situations from now on.

RELAXATION

Another very valuable positive resource Key is the *relaxation Key*. With this Key, every time you fire it off your body will be filled with warm, relaxing feelings. You can remember times when you felt relaxed and Key those feelings in. You can also Key in the feelings you have just before you fall asleep at night. Key those feelings in and take that relaxation Key wherever you go. People have used the relaxation Key to end *insomnia* in just one night! You can also use this Key for an instant relaxation break in the middle of the day when needed.

CURIOSITY AND WONDER

There's a resource Key I like very much and it's the *curiousity and wonder Key*. We were born with curiosity and wonder in our genes and I think the best state is to return to that childlike wonder. Do you remember times when you were a kid filled with those feelings of wonder. Such feelings as, "Wow look, there's a bug! I wonder what's over there? Wow, look at that cloud, amazing!" Can you recall those childhood feelings of curiosity, amazement and wonder? As you do, Key them in, stack the Key and make it strong. Perhaps you can the wake up each morning full of wonder and curiosity as to what the day will bring. Maybe you'll start the day with, as I recommend to everyone, "I wonder, I wonder what wonderful thing is going to happen today! I wonder!"

OTHER EXAMPLES OF "KEYING"

One time there was a little girl who was watching television and she saw a monstrous, horrible movie. The movie made such an impact on her nerves that she started having trouble sleeping at night. She also became afraid of going to school. She would actually walk down the middle of the street because she thought the monsters were going to pop out from behind the bushes and trees. I had her Key in a calm, relaxed yet alert state.

Then, as she held that Key and felt those calm, relaxed and alert feelings she, her mother, and I walked down the middle of the street washing away the negative, fearful feelings that were associated with the bushes and the monsters in her mind. After this, she found she could go to sleep more easily and she could go to school quite comfortably. Those negative, fearful feelings had been washed away completely and permanently.

Another area where the Keying process works very well is in sports and *peak performance.* I have worked with many athletes who came to see me because they were overly anxious. They would get tense and suddenly they couldn't perform. They would "choke", or they would go into a slump. And as with professionals, often these reactions seriously affected their careers.

I have had those athletes remember times when they performed at the peak of their ability. When they got those prior feelings of top, *peak performance* they would Key them in. They would stack the Key and make it stronger and stronger. They were able to use that Key in situations which would normally cause them to "choke". When needed, they would fire off that *peak performance Key.* Those exciting, resourceful peak performance physical feelings would automatically be replayed.

These athletes have found they were able to perform at their best more often for longer periods of time and were able to feel calmer and more confident while they were doing it.

Suppose you could use a Key for dieting. It's not only possible, it works. I guarantee it. One fellow came to see me who couldn't stay on his diet. He really wanted to lose weight. His doctor had told him that he should lose weight. He would try to use positive thinking and he would to try to use will power. He would lose a few pounds, then suddenly gorge out and stuff himself and quickly gain all of the weight back.

I had him remember those times when he felt completely stuffed and very uncomfortable. Then I had him Key in those stuffed, full feelings. Every time before he sat down to a meal, or he felt like going off his diet, he would fired off his stuffed Key. Suddenly he felt full and had no desire to overeat. Just by using the

Keying process, he was able to stay on his diet without excessive will power or without struggle.

It is impossible to overemphasize how important and how powerful the Keying process is. It can wash away fear and negative feelings. It can give you positive, powerful feelings that you can replay at will and use in any situation. With the Keying process, you are well on your way to a life of more personal power.

What's so exciting is you can use Keying to give you the feelings you want in any future situation. A techniques called *future pacing* will allow you to have *any* situation be the trigger for the feelings you want or need!

Let's go to the next chapter and take a look.

CHAPTER V.

YOU NEVER HAVE TO HAVE ANOTHER BAD DAY

LOCKING IN POSITIVE FEELINGS FOR ANY FUTURE SITUATION

How would you like to be able to program yourself to feel and act any way you want automatically? How would you like to have a situation that that has always made you afraid or upset instead, create positive powerful feelings in you?

What's being suggested is called *future pacing*. Future pacing is a way to program yourself to think, feel and act the way you want to, in any future situation, more predictably and automatically.

Future pacing is important to use with all of the Keying techniques you are learning because it will program you to automatically remember to use the techniques in other places and at other times when they will be most useful.

STATE-DEPENDENT LEARNING

Have you ever noticed that you might learn something in a certain place and when you leave that place, you forget just about everything you learned? This is called "state-dependent learning". Students often have this problem. They know it all in the classroom, but they can't use the knowledge anywhere else.

Future pacing insures that you will be able to remember and utilize the valuable learnings and understandings, from Keying, in any future situation at any future time, automatically.

Future pacing gives you control over your learning ability that is yet another step beyond visualizing, positive thinking and beyond any previously known technique. With future pacing you can consciously control state-dependent learning easily and predictably.

Future pacing can be used to cause a future situation that would normally trigger negative feelings, or negative behavior, to be the very Key to trigger off new and positive desired feelings automatically. Future pacing is a way in which you can program yourself to be the way you want to be in *any* future situation.

When Evelyn first came to see me she was ready to quit school. She was studying communications and every time she had to speak before her class, she worried about it for weeks. When she got up in front of the class to speak, her voice would crack, her legs would shake so much she thought she was going to fall down.

I asked, "Evelyn, how do you want to feel? How do you want to feel when you talk in front of a group of people?" She said, "I want to feel calm and alert." I asked, "How about a little bit excited, too?" She laughed and said that would be wonderful. I had her remember some different times when she felt calm, alert and had those excited feelings. We Keyed them in and got a good strong Key of her desired state.

Then I had Evelyn fire off her Key and when she got those calm, alert, excited feelings I had her see herself, in the future, feeling those positive feelings talking to groups of people. I had her see herself in the near future, then, a couple of months in the future, and then, two years in the future.

I, then, had her think of all those future experiences again. This time entering the scene "as if" she were there. I had her go into the "associated state" all the while holding her calm, alert Key feeling calm, relaxed and assured. When she was finished, I had her let go of her Key, and imagine talking to the class. She said, "Dr. Dossey, I can't believe it. It's amazing. I'm actually looking forward to doing it!"

Just the thought of speaking now triggers off calm and excited feelings in Evelyn. Since then, Evelyn has been successfully speaking in front of large groups for years.

STEPS IN FUTURE PACING

Let's do a future pacing activity. You may want to refer to the page entitled "Future Pacing" as you go along.

Think of some future activity you want to do, some future situation that gives you an anxious, negative feeling when you think about doing it. A feeling that you would like to change.

Maybe you have to do something in the future and you don't feel motivated to do it and you would like to feel motivated. Or maybe that future situation makes you feel fearful and you would rather feel more confident and assured when you think of doing it, or when actually doing it.

FUTURE PACING

Purpose: To cause a future situation that would normally trigger old negative feelings and behavior to be the "cue" or trigger for new, desired feelings and behavior automatically.

To shorten the rehearsal process.

To create future control of the Think/Feel/Do/Have Motivation and Success Formula.

STEPS IN FUTURE PACING

1. Acknowledge the current situation.
2. Give thanks for the "problem."
3. Determine desired state or behavior you want in the future situation.
4. Key in the desired feelings.
5. Test the Key to be sure it's strong.
6. Fire off the desired feeling Key and see yourself in the future doing the new behavior.
7. Then check to see if the new behavior is what you really want in the future situation. If it is, continue. If not, return to Step 3 and create a different desired state.
8. Holding your Key, begin with 12 hours in future seeing yourself doing the desired behavior. Progress to 3 days, one week, three months, etc., into the future, DISSOCIATED.
9. Repeat Step 8 in ASSOCIATED state. Jump into the pictures and be in the future picture, doing the new behavior and feeling the desired feelings.
10. Ecological check. Find a future situation where it would be appropriate to maintain the old behavior.
11. Test. Think of that future situation and notice the difference in your thoughts and feelings.
12. Get out of the way and keep your eyes open for the Deli Signs!

Think of that future situation you want to change your feelings about, and notice how you feel.

STEP ONE in future pacing is to simply acknowledge your feelings about that particular situation, just the way they are. You don't have to understand or analyze those feelings. This is not psychotherapy. Just think about the future situation and notice how you feel about it.

STEP TWO. Give thanks for the problem. Keep in mind, you don't really have any "problems". Problems are simply the result of looking at things through the Problem Frame. When we reframe a problem by using the Outcome Frame, the problem becomes a challenging opportunity that is put in front of us so we can exercise our creativity. Just give thanks for the opportunity.

STEP THREE. Decide what you want to feel instead. When you see yourself in that situation, how would you like to feel? Let's say you would like to feel confident and assured. Then you can fire off your confidence Key.

If you would like to feel more motivated or if you would like to feel more relaxed or creative, then use the Keying process to Key in those feelings as your desired state. That's **STEP FOUR.** Do that now.

Now that you have created a strong desired state of confidence and Keyed it in, you want to test that Key. That is **STEP FIVE.** Test you Key. Fire off the Key and feel those desired feelings. As long as you are holding that Key you will continue to feel those feelings.

In **STEPS SIX** and **SEVEN,** as you feel those desired "as if" feelings, look at the future situation on your mental screen and ask yourself, "Are these the feelings I *really want* to have in this upcoming situation? Is this the *appropriate* behavior I want to have in this future situation?"

This check is to make sure the new resources, and the new "as if" feelings, and the new behavior you are creating for that future situation are really the ones that will serve you the best.

If yes, you will get a definite sense of "yes", this is the resource, these are the feelings and behavior I want to have. They will get the results I'm after. If not, this resource is not right for this situation.

If you do get a "no", go back and think of other resources you would like to have in that future situation that *would* get the results you want more specifically. Creativity perhaps, or calm and relaxed, for example. Then, Key those in.

However, when you do get a "yes" answer, as you are sitting in the audience looking at your mental screen, holding your Key, feeling the feelings that you want to have in that future situation, go on to step number eight.

STEP EIGHT is, from the audience's point of view, holding your Key, watch yourself on the screen in your future situation. See yourself 12 hours in the future feeling the way you want to feel in that situation, acting the way you want to act in that situation. Run the scene a little bit. See yourself doing those things you want to do. You don't have to complete it all. Remember, the unconscious mind will fill in the gaps.

Now, see yourself, say, three days in the future, doing the things you want to be doing, the way you want to be doing them, still holding your positive resource Key. Hold those good "as if" feelings as you watch yourself in the future, feeling the way you want to feel, and doing what you want to do.

Now, imagine yourself a week into the future and see yourself doing those same things, and feeling those good "as if" feelings as you're doing them.

Okay, let's take a big leap in time. See yourself three months from now. Feeling the way you want to feel in that situation, doing the things you want to do in that situation. Now, let's go even farther into the future. Still holding the Key, still feeling those desired feelings, in the desired state, see yourself in that situation a year in the future, feeling the way you feel now, and doing what you want to be doing in that situation.

STEP NINE. Still holding your positive resource Key, see yourself on the screen again, 12 hours in the future in that same situation. This time, enter your body on the screen, and allow yourself to be "in" the situation "as if" you were really there mentally and physically engaged in the associated state. You are "in" the movie now — no longer watching from the audience.

Hold your Key and now feel the way you want to feel. If you can, actually act the way you want to act in that situation. Great. Now jump ahead to one week in the future. Be in the situation, feeling the way you want to feel, doing what you want to do.

Now, go farther into the future. It's three months in the future. You are holding your Key, you are feeling those good "as if" feelings and you are actually doing what you want to do in that situation. Good. Now jump ahead a year in that situation, feeling those feelings, doing what you want to do.

Now go to **STEP TEN.** Let's do what is called an "ecological check". Think of that future situation again and imagine a time when it would be appropriate for you to have your old unwanted feelings about it.

For example, I had a man one time who was afraid to drive on the freeway. Every time he even thought about driving on the freeway, he felt afraid. I used the future pacing process with him. When we were finished, his thinking about driving on the freeway actually triggered off the feelings of confidence in him. Instead of triggering fear, he automatically felt confident.

Then I did the *ecological check*. I asked him, "Christopher, can you imagine any time when driving on the freeway when you would want to be afraid?" He thought and said, "Yes." Remember, fear can also be a protective response, it can keep us alert, it can keep us out of trouble and safe. So I had him think of a time when being a little nervous and still being alert on the freeway would be an appropriate way to be. When it was appropriate for him to feel anxious yet alert.

So, think about your future situation. Find one time in the future when it would be a good idea to have your unwanted feelings or your old behavior. Good, just note and acknowledge that. That's all you have to do.

The ecological check adds to your flexibility. It programs your brain and body so that you are able to respond in the future with an entire range of appropriate feelings and behaviors. Your choices range all the way from the negative feelings you had originally, to the new positive feelings you have created in the future pacing activity.

STEP ELEVEN. Test your programming. Without firing off your Key, think about going into that situation and notice how differently you think and feel. Another way to test your work is to actually go into that situation and see how you feel and do.

STEP TWELVE. Get out of the way and keep your eyes open for those Deli Signs.

Keep your eyes open because, in the most unusual places, to your surprise and amazement, you will find yourself doing things that you wanted to do. You'll feel the way you wanted to feel, without even thinking about it. Often times, you will find yourself looking back and noticing you have already done the thing you were afraid of before. You felt fine and you acted in a positive resourceful way. Then often you'll think, "My goodness, look at that. Future pacing really is powerful!"

Perhaps you have already noticed one thing that is not only interesting but very important. When you are future pacing and creating your future state, you are following exactly the same steps that you used to create the Outcome Frame.

When you use the *Outcome Frame,* and when you use the *future pacing* process, you are creating new neurological pathways and new patterns of thinking in your brain and body. These will lead you automatically to think, to feel and to act in more positive, creative, satisfying and successful ways. Future pacing sets up a conscious and unconscious trajectory, or aim, toward your desired outcome.

This works in two ways. First, it causes you to think and act in ways that automatically propel you toward your outcome. And second, it allows you to see and use those very things already in the external world, already in your mind and body, those Deli Signs. Those very things you need to achieve the results you want.

APPLICATIONS OF FUTURE PACING

What a powerful tool *future pacing* is. Just imagine being able to program yourself to feel and act in just the way you want in any future situation and then have it happen automatically and predictably.

Future pacing works very well with *dieting*. You can simply Key in feelings of motivation and then see yourself on your mental screen being motivated to eat healthily and being motivated to leave the table when you have had enough. You can see yourself being motivated to walk past the refrigerator. Then, you can see yourself eating appropriately and stopping when full. Not wishing it were so, but actually feeling it is so, with the Key.

By seeing and feeling yourself becoming thinner and healthier as you future pace into the future, you can actually make eating itself your Key to trigger off the feelings of motivation to eat appropriately. Then you will eat to live not live to eat.

Many people use future pacing to help them in their careers. You may have a project that you have wanted to do or some work that you have to do and you don't feel motivated to do it. Or maybe you feel fearful when thinking about doing it.

As you did before, first Key in those strong feelings of *motivation* and *assuredness*, and then, see yourself in the future, handling the project the way you want to handle it, doing the work you need to do. Feeling powerful, motivated and confident. With future pacing you are actually programming your brain and body so that your work or the project itself becomes the Key that triggers off the feelings of motivation and excitement you need in order to do the work. It works beautifully.

Another powerful way to use future pacing is for *relaxation* and *resourcefulness*. Often, you may find yourself in a particular situation or experience that makes you feel stressful, or makes you feel tense and anxious. Key in calm, relaxed, purposeful feelings and then see yourself in the future meeting those situations, having those experiences you want. By doing that, you will have programmed yourself so that the future situation will no longer trigger stress in you. Rather, that situation itself will be the new Key that actually triggers off and replays those feelings of relaxation and resourcefulness.

You may be asking,"What about *personal relationships*? Will future pacing work to better relationships?" Of course, and in a powerful, and effective way, too.

How would you like to feel and act when you are with your loved ones, those people who are important in your life? Maybe you don't always feel and act the way you'd like when you are with them. It happens to all of us at times.

You can use the Keying process to Key in the feelings you would like to have with those people close to you. Then, see yourself in the future, feeling those good feelings you want to feel. See yourself acting the way you want to act when being with those you love in the way you want to be with them. Feeling warmly and lovingly. You can program yourself to feel and act the way you truly want towards those you love. Future pacing can work miracles in relationships.

Again, more often than not, when people use the future Pace technique for something, they will then go out into the world and automatically do the things they future paced. They feel the feelings they future paced, but are not even aware they're feeling them at the time.

Perhaps you too will find, to your amazement and surprise, those feelings and actions you have future paced will happen automatically. You won't even notice until after it happens and you will look back and say, "How curious and amazing. It happened just the way I wanted, and without my even being aware of it. Future pacing really works!"

Future pacing will allow you to look forward to those

situations which, in the past, normally triggered old behavior. These situations will become your cue, your trigger, your Key for new and desired behavior, for a new and desired life.

Perhaps you have your favorite *affirmations, visualizations,* or *prayers* you could now make even more predictable by using them with your future pacing technique.

Now, use your "Generalizing and Future Programing" activity with future pacing before you go into the next section.

Let's now take a look at how the Key and the Keying process can be used to let go of the past, wash away blocks and barriers and give us even more flexibility.

CHAPTER VI.

CURING THE ADDICTION
TO UNHAPPINESS —

WASHING AWAY FEARS,
PHOBIAS, AND STRESS FOREVER

Y ou have just learned a way to prepare yourself to have any feelings you want in any future situations. How to have more options, more increased flexibility you desire and deserve. There are additional ways to use Keying to increase your flexibility. These are techniques called "Collapsing the Keys", the "Two Place Wash" and the "Three Place Wash".

UNLOCK BLOCKS AND BARRIERS THAT ARE KEEPING YOU FROM DOING WHAT YOU KNOW YOU CAN DO.

COLLAPSING "KEYS"

Collapsing Keys is another powerful and fast way to

collapse and eliminate negative Keys and negative feelings and replace them with positive Keys and positive feelings. Collapsing Keys is useful in a wide variety of ways.

As we have been learning, our lives are filled with Keys, positive Keys, negative Keys. We cannot not Key. We are always Keying. Keying is going on constantly and our feelings, our emotions — even our actions — are affected by these Keys all the time.

Have you ever started to suddenly feel bad? All of a sudden, for some unknown reason, have you ever begun to feel uncomfortable and you didn't even know what was causing it? Well, if you had examined it carefully, you would perhaps have noticed that the bad feelings were triggered by some negative Key. Our own children can become negative Keys to us. Our workplace can become a negative Key. Our homes or our cars can become negative Keys.

To have more personal power, you need ways to eliminate negative Keys from your life and replace them with positive ones so that you can feel the way you want to feel.

Collapsing Keys is a quick and effective way to do just that. When you learn to collapse Keys, you can erase negative Keys and their effects and replace them with positive Keys. Keys that give you positive feelings and consequently the results you want in life. In short, you can start taking more control.

A man named Tim who was a writer for a major movie studio in Southern California came to see me. He had a terrible case of what's called "writer's block". That is, whenever he tried to work on his current project, he got stuck. He was blocked. He could not create or produce any productive thoughts when he sat down to write. And it was getting worse.

I said, "Tim, hold out your right hand. We are going to make your right hand your desired state Key. When you sit down to write, how do you want to feel and be?" And he said to me, "Dr. Dossey, I want to feel and be more creative." He had felt creative many times in the past so I had him remember those times. When he was feeling those creative feelings, I had him hold out his right hand with the palm up and shake his right hand gently. With that hand movement as a key he Keyed those feelings in.

I had him go to a neutral state and said, "Tim, how did those blocked feelings feel when you would sit down and write?" He said, "They felt terrible. I felt frustrated, tense, and afraid." When I saw he was really feeling those unwanted feelings, I had him hold his left hand out, palm upward and shake it gently. We Keyed all those negative feelings into the left hand.

Then I said, "Tim, we are going to do something called collapsing Keys. I want you to hold out both of your hands, palms upward, the positive and the negative, and shake them both gently at the same time." What I was doing was having him fire off his positive and negative Keys simultaneously! As he did, his face first looked confused, and in a short period of time his face and body became relaxed.

He dropped his hands and looked at me and I asked, "Now, how do you feel when you think about writing?" He thought about it and he said, "That's amazing, Dr. Dossey, I don't feel tense anymore. I feel fine about it. I feel like the creative juices are flowing again."

Then I did a quick future pace with him. I asked, "Tim, can you fire off your positive Key." He did. "Now can you see yourself tomorrow, writing, creating, feeling good?" He said, "Yes." I future paced him three months into the future and then a year into the future. That was the end of his writer's block!

It was so simple. Before Tim collapsed the Keys, he was completely controlled by his negative Key. The best he could feel when he tried to write was stuck and frustrated and blocked.

Because he had collapsed the Keys however, he had opened up a whole range of possible feelings from the negative Key of being frustrated and stuck to the positive Key of feeling extremely creative and excited. Now, when he sits down to write, Tim can feel anything within that entire range of feelings.

Is it now possible for him to still feel stuck and blocked? Yes, but it's an interesting phenomenon that when the human organism has a range of choices, a range of feelings and behavior from which to choose, it always chooses the best one.

So when Tim sits down to write, because it is now possible for him to feel creative and challenged, that is what his body and brain automatically choose to feel. He automatically makes the best choice.

STEPS IN COLLAPSING "KEYS"

Collapsing keys is so simple. Let's review the five basic steps. Step one, acknowledge the negative situation. Two, Key in the feelings you want to feel on one hand. Three, Key in the way you already feel, the negative state, on the other hand. Four, fire off both Keys simultaneously. Five, future pace and keep your eyes open, for the Deli Signs!

GUIDED ACTIVITY IN UNLOCKING BARRIERS — COLLAPSING "KEYS"

Let's do a collapsing Keys activity.

First look at the page marked "Activity Performance Check". This *Self Test* is easy and exciting to use.

ACTIVITY PERFORMANCE CHECK

A SELF TEST
(Before and After)

I. **List the negative feeling and/or behavior to be changed.**

_____

II. **Pre-Test**

Scale the negative feeling or behavior (0 being least intense and 10 being most intense)

0   1   2   3   4   5   6   7   8   9   10
Pre-State Test

III. **Desired State**

Scale the desired feeling you want instead.

0   1   2   3   4   5   6   7   8   9   10
Desired State

IV. **Post-Test**

After completing your activity, scale the feeling again and notice the difference.

0   1   2   3   4   5   6   7   8   9   10
Post-State Test

V. **What's Next?**

Write down your determined next step. _____

_____

It will help measure the positive results that any Keying process creates for you.

First, note the negative feeling or behavior you'd like to change and on a scale from 1 to 10, one being the least intense and 10 the most intense, scale your present intensity level.

After you do that, go through the collapsing Keys activity and when you have completed it, return to this page and on the Post Test, scale the intensity of your results. Notice the change in your feelings. Many people like to use this check before and after each activity.

Now, let's do the collapsing Keys activity.

For your positive state Key, gently hold out your right hand palm up and gently shake it, just like Tim did. And for your negative Key, use your left hand and do the same thing.

First, think of a situation or a person who gives you a negative feeling, one you want to change. Maybe some particular thing makes you feel angry or stuck like Tim was. Just identify and acknowledge that situation. Then, write it down on your Self Test in the space provided.

Start from your neutral state. Let's create the negative state Key. Think of the negative situation. Let yourself feel the negative feelings that you've been feeling when you think about that situation or that person. When you are feeling those negative feelings strongly, gently shake your left hand. Good. Now think about that situation again or that person again and feel those negative feelings again. When you are feeling them strongly, gently shake your left hand again.

Now from your neutral state, test that Key and scale those feelings.

Now, let's determine your desired state. How do you want to feel instead? Confident? Relaxed? Motivated? Loving?

Remember a time when you had those strong positive feelings and when you were feeling the way you want to feel very strongly. As you begin to feel those feelings, gently shake your right hand, Keying those feelings in. Keep stacking that key until you have Keyed in good strong positive feelings by shaking your right hand gently.

Now go to your neutral state. Test your Key and scale your feelings.

Go to your neutral state again. Now, at the same time, hold out your left hand and your right hand in the same position, and gently shake them both the same way for about 30 seconds to a minute or until you feel a sense of integration. You will feel more together. It's a sense of completeness and you will automatically begin to focus outside of yourself.

Let's do a quick future pace so you will be able to have this positive result in the future. Shake your right hand gently to get those positive feelings back. If they aren't as strong as you want them to be now, just stack the Key some more. Can you imagine a time in the near future when these positive feelings will be of value to you? Good. Can you think of another time in a more distant future when these feelings will be useful? A situation when these positive feelings can be helpful to you? Key that in.

Now test your results. Refer back to your Self Test and notice the change in your feelings. Isn't that amazing! Collapsing Keys can be used for almost anything.

OTHER APPLICATIONS OF COLLAPSING "KEYS"

I can't really think of anything that collapsing Keys cannot be used for. If you have habits you don't like and you want to do something differently, collapsing Keys is an excellent tool for that.

Collapsing Keys is also powerful and effective in *relationships*. As I mentioned before, very often, we become negative Keys for our loved ones and they for us.

In that situation, you simply need to acknowledge the situation, then Key in the way you want to feel with your loved one with one Key. Key in the way you do feel with your loved one, with another Key.

Then, fire off both keys simultaneously and you will wash away that negative Key and replace it with more positive choices.

For example, let's say you feel "out of love" with someone you really want to have loving and caring feelings for. Ask yourself, how do I want to feel instead? Think of times when you had those loving feelings (Not wishful loving feelings but, "as if" loving feelings). When you get those feelings of love and caring, Key them in.

Then, Key in those unloving feelings with a different Key. Then fire off both Keys simultaneously and notice how you can build good feelings of love and caring back into your relationship.

Collapsing Keys is a fast and effective way to get rid of fears and *phobias*. Does something make you feel afraid? Key in the way you want to feel. Key in the fearful feelings. Fire off both Keys simultaneously and you will wash away the fear, just like the ocean waves wash away the footprints in the sand.

Collapsing Keys can also be used to *expand your com-*

fort zone. Remember, when you have changes in your life that take you out of your range of familiar, comfortable feelings, you may tend to do things to bring yourself back into your level of familiarity, your comfort zone. That means, if you are feeling too happy, or too successful, or too powerful, you might unconsciously sabotage your own success.

So you can collapse Keys when you want to *expand your comfort zone*, when you want to enjoy more love, enjoy more happiness, and enjoy more creativity. When you want to enjoy more personal power. You can do all of this now comfortably and predictably.

Here's an example of expanding the comfort zone. Let's say you get a promotion or a new job with new responsibilities, more money, more challenge. Maybe some excessive fear and uncomfortableness is there, too. The operative questions to asked are, "How do I want to feel in my new job? How do I want to feel having more money?" Create, and Key in those positive desired feelings.

Then make another Key for the negative feelings that you do have. Fire off both Keys simultaneously and wash away the negative Key. Remember to future pace and keep your eyes open for the Deli Signs!

Refer to the page entitled "Collapsing Keys". This chart will help you reinforce the ideas you have just learned.

Let's talk about the importance of quickly future pacing all the techniques and learnings as you go along. I feel so strongly about it that I think it should become a habit for all new learnings in life.

At the end of the activity you did on Collapsing Keys, for example, I had you go into the immediate future holding your positive Key and seeing yourself with the new positive resources. Then, I had you think of a more

COLLAPSING "KEYS"

Creating a New Range of Choices
of Feelings and Actions

Purpose:

1. To increase flexibility and choices in behavior.

2. To cancel preexisting negative Keys.

3. To unlock blocks and barriers or stuck behaviors

STEPS IN COLLAPSING "KEYS"

1. Identify your unwanted feelings/behavior.

2. Create the unwanted state, Key it in. Test it.

3. Create your desired state and Key it in. Then. test it.

4. Fire off both Keys at the same time. Hold until you feel a sense of integration (30 to 60 seconds).

5. Test the process by firing off your undesired state Key and notice the change in your feelings.

6. Do a quick Future Pace.

7. Test by imagining the situation and notice your new feelings.

— COLLAPSING KEYS —

Present State   Desired State

Negative Feelings,   Positive Feelings,
Responses or Behavior   Responses or Behavior

This is your new range of possible feeling and action

distant time in the future when the positive feelings would be of value. That is a very fast version of the future pacing process.

It programs these new changes to stay with you in future situations and at future times. And they will be there for you to use. It is very important that you do a quick future pace at the end of each new learning and understanding you gain from this book or anywhere else in your life for that matter.

As you see and feel yourself in the future using the new skills and information you have acquired, you literally program your brain and body to make that skill or information available to you in future times and future places automatically. The unconscious fills in the gaps.

Future pacing is like instructing your brain and your body to file your new knowledge, your new feelings and behavior for future reference.

Have you ever wondered whether you can truly let go of the past? Let's go to the next section and see how.

LOCKING OUT NEGATIVE FEELINGS ASSOCIATED WITH THE PAST

THE TWO PLACE WASH

The *two place wash* is an extremely powerful technique. It allows you to use the Key to change your feelings about past events forever. This, in turn, changes your expectations and feelings about the future. People use the two place wash to free themselves from negative feelings of fear caused by past experiences, and to expand their possibilities for the future.

A young 14 year old boy named Kenny came to see me a while back and he had what's called "test anxiety". He was bright enough but was afraid to take tests in school, so his grades were going down. I taught him the confidence Key just like you've learned. Then, when he took a test, he fired off his confidence Key and it worked fine. He felt more confident taking tests and his grades improved greatly.

Some time later, Kenny came into the office and asked, "Dr. Dossey, will this confidence Key work when I ask a girl for a date?" I could see he was getting embarrassed and uncomfortable even talking to me about it.

He told me he had asked a girl out on a date and she'd turned him down while some of his friends were standing around and they gave him a hard time about it. Then, every time he even thought about asking a girl out, he would get so shy and embarrassed and tense in his body, that he couldn't even open his mouth to speak. His negative feelings were a little too strong for a simple Key, or a collapsing Keys, so I decided to teach him something different.

I asked Kenny, "How would you like to wash away those horrible feelings you have when you think of asking that girl for a date? He smiled and said, "Sure!"

"Well," I said, "I'm going to do a two place wash with you. First, fire off your confidence Key right now." Kenny reached over and he touched his left wrist and in a couple of seconds I could see his body begin to relax, his breathing changed, and he sat up straighter in his chair.

Then, I said, "Now Kenny, still holding your Key, I want you to imagine that you are in a movie theatre sitting in the audience. Imagine you are looking at a movie screen and on the movie screen, there is a movie of you when you asked that girl out on a date."

He said okay, and I told him, "Keep holding your Key, feeling confident. Remember to stay in the audience. We're going to put a wedge in between your thoughts and feelings." He said alright. Then, I said, "Okay, now watch yourself in the movie asking that girl out on a date, getting rejected. Keep holding your confidence Key and feeling those confident feelings. As you do that how do you feel?"

He said, "I feel fine Dr. Dossey." I said, "Great, now run the movie backwards." He did. Then, I said, "Run the movie forward again very fast. When you get to the end of the scene, run the movie backwards very fast." He did it and then, I said, "Now, turn the picture upside down and show the movie upside down and forward, all the time holding your confidence key. Now run the movie upside down and backwards." He did that, then I said, "Great Kenny."

After having him go into his neutral state I said, "Alright Kenny, notice how you feel now thinking about asking that girl for a date, or any girl for a date." He thought about it for a little while, then he looked at me and began to get a great big smile on his face. He said, "I feel just fine. That's amazing Dr. Dossey!" The negative feelings had been washed away!

I spoke to Kenny a few months after that and I asked him how he felt about asking girls out on dates. He smiled real big and said not only was he having no problems, but he was even teaching the confidence Key and the two place wash to some of his friends at school.

What Kenny did with the two place wash was he changed forever his feelings about a past experience. He diluted and washed away and changed his negative physical nerve pathways. You could say he actually changed his personal history. That's what we are going to do right now.

STEPS IN TWO PLACE WASH

1. Identify unwanted feelings/behavior. Scale intensity on Self Test.

2. Key in undesirable feelings.

3. Key in positive resources (D/S).

4. Dissociate — Hold positive Key and review three negative past experiences. Or view upside down, back and forth, etc.

5. Associate — Repeat steps number three and four.

6. Test and scale the results.

7. Future pace with appropriate ecological check.

8. Keep eyes open for Deli Signs!

THE TWO PLACE WASH

Purpose:

1. To free yourself of negative feelings associated with past traumas.

2. To wash away negative habits.

WEDGE
TWO PLACE WASH

Thinking about past situation produces Negative Feelings

Thinking about the situation produces Neutral or Positive Feelings.
Holding Positive Key

I want to guide you through the steps of the two place wash. This will allow you to free yourself of any negative feelings you may have that are associated with past experiences and traumas.

STEPS IN TWO PLACE WASH — GUIDED ACTIVITY

First look at the page marked "Activity Performance Check". Note the negative feeling or behavior you'd like to change. On a scale from 1 to 10, one being the least intense and 10 the most intense, scale your present intensity level.

After you do that, go through the wash, return to this page and, on the post test, scale the intensity of your results. Notice the change in your feelings.

Now, let's do the wash.

The first thing I'd like you to do is remember a past situation or experience that makes you feel bad. Not really horrible, we don't want to go for the big one yet.

Just think of some experience in your past, some situation that gives you a negative feeling when you think about it. Perhaps something that makes you a little fearful or disgusts you a little bit, or makes you a little angry, or sad. That's the one. Now scale that feeling on your Self Test if you haven't already done so.

Now, go into your neutral state, focus outside yourself, shake your body around a little bit. Good. Now imagine you are sitting in the audience of a movie theatre, and as you are sitting there, reach over and fire off your confidence Key.

Give those feelings of confidence a second or two to develop and build. Now as you are feeling those confident feelings strongly, watch the memory movie of yourself going through that uncomfortable experience or being in that uncomfortable situation.

Watch it like a movie. All the while, staying in the audience, holding your confidence Key, feeling those feelings of confidence, watch the scene until the negative experience is over and then stop the movie.

Now run the movie backwards. Still holding the confidence Key, run the movie forward again. Watch the scene again in fast motion. Fast forward. Now run the scene backwards very quickly. Rewind the film.

Next, turn the movie upside down and watch the scene again upside down and forward. Take as much time as you need. Now run it upside down and backwards. Good. (An effective option is, while in the audience, view three past events when you felt and experienced the unwanted feelings.)

Okay, now go to your neutral state. Jiggle your body a little bit, focus out the window, or on a picture on the wall or think of something else.

Now, without firing off your confidence Key, simply think of that negative experience or that situation again and notice the difference in your feelings. Scale it on a scale from 1 to 10. Then, when you think of that situation, compare the feelings you have now to the feelings you felt before you did the two place wash. Isn't that amazing!

GENERALIZING YOUR LEARNING FOR DEEPER PROGRAMING

Now with the information that you have learned so far, the Keying process, the confidence Key, Collapsing Keys and the Two Place Wash, can you think of a time when any one of those would have been valuable in the past? Just think of one time in your past when this information would have been valuable.

Perhaps, you can think of when this information might be valuable for you in the future. Imagine one time in the near future, and in the long term future when the two place wash and the confidence Key and the Keying process could be valuable to you.

The two place wash is a very powerful technique. It can be used to wash away the negative effects of any past experience in all areas of life: work, career, social, financial and in the area of relationships. These negative effects also create ineffective habits and future expectations that can be washed and changed. When the habits and fears or traumas of the past are extremely severe you can use the three place wash.

LETTING GO OF THE PAST — WASHING AWAY SEVERE PHOBIAS AND TRAUMAS

THE "THREE PLACE WASH"

The *three place wash* is really the most powerful, the most effective technique known to wash away the effects of *severe past traumas* that are limiting your life now.

If you have a severe fear or a *phobia*, this is the technique you want. It is the activity to be used when a person has been *raped, mugged, beaten or abused* or severely traumatized. I call the three place wash the miracle process because of its power to get results. When collapsing Keys and the two place wash don't quite get you the results you want, the three place wash will.

You can refer to your "Fear and Phobia Finder" in the back of your book for a complete list of more than 250 fears and phobias which this process can eliminate quickly, easily and painlessly, and permanently.

As we all know, the biggest limiter of human life is fear. The biggest destroyer of hopes, plans and dreams is fear — to say nothing of the physical damage to our bodies. Fear makes us feel smaller than we are. It makes our lives seem smaller and less colorful, less fulfilling and much more painful. Nothing drains the joy and heart and zest from life like fear.

Fear affects all of us to one degree or another and

at one time or another. We have been learning in this program, how programmable we human beings are and how none of us survived childhood without learning to fear one thing or another. We have all been, in the course of growing up, abused or traumatized in some way, physically or psychologically, whether we know it or not. It is not easy growing up. For some, it can be a very frightening thing.

Some people can remember horrible, traumatic experiences from their past and they know what "caused" their fears. But many people are not even aware of the source of their fear. They don't know where it came from, they are not sure when it even started. They only know they are afraid and it hurts and the pain and fear is with them everyday. They spend a great deal of their life just trying to avoid it, or worse yet, just living with it.

Well it doesn't have to be that way anymore. And it doesn't matter whether you remember the cause of the fear. The three place wash works just as well.

It's extremely powerful with all anxieties, fears and phobias because what a fear actually is is the result of a negative Key. A Key that produces a strong negative feeling response. It may be a memory Key that produces those negative feelings.

The Key may be the thought of flying in an airplane, if you are afraid of airplanes and flying. Or, the key could be the sight of a dog if you are afraid of dogs. It could be the thought of failure or success or the fear of relationships. It could be a smell. Whatever it is, there is a negative Key there somewhere.

Remember, you were born with only two fears. The fear of falling and the fear of loud noises. You were not born with the fear of failure or the fear of success or the fear of intimacy or the fear of being alone. You were not born with the fear of elevators or highways or insects. You were not born with the fear of open spaces or closed spaces.

All of those fears have been learned. Any fear you may have was Keyed into you. When you do the three place wash, you will wash away the negative feeling associated with that Key. Then, when you think about that particular fearful thing or situation, your body just does not feel those fearful feelings anymore. Consequently, your expectations and your feelings about the future will also change forever.

One important thing about the three place wash. It also works on any other unwanted feelings beside fears. It works on any negative feeling left over from the past whether we are aware of the feeling being fear based or not.

Maybe you are holding on to hurts and resentments toward someone because of the past and you're having difficulty forgiving. Perhaps you are hanging on to old hurts and emotional bruises from a current relationship.

You might be hanging on to grief or mourning that is excessive or prolonged. You could be hanging onto a broken heart or you may be excessively jealous of someone.

The three place wash is extremely effective in freeing you of any of those old negative Keys and painful feelings. It is a predictable, easy way to let go of the past forever; to free you from suffering the negative effects of the past; to open up your life and give you new choices for the future.

STEPS IN THE THREE PLACE WASH

As I go through the steps in the three place wash, I want you to personally go through it just like you would in my audio cassette programs and seminars.

You can refer to the page that has the listed steps entitled "The Three Place Wash".

To test your results of the three place wash, use another Activity Performance Check sheet. This pre and post test will once again give you a way to measure the results and effectiveness of a particular technique, and will tell you what to do next.

The three place wash is similar to the two place wash we did earlier. The three place wash also takes place in your mental movie theater.

However, instead of sitting only in the audience watching yourself on the movie screen, you will also imagine yourself sitting in a projection booth watching yourself in the audience. You watch yourself, watching yourself on the movie screen.

First. think of the negative feeling that you want to wash away. Do not go for the big one right now. Just choose a situation that makes you feel mildly fearful or uncomfortable. After you have learned the three place wash, then you can use it for even the most terrifying and severest of fears. But for the first time through, it's best to choose a milder fear.

Once you have identified that unwanted state, step two is to establish a positive resource Key. Ask yourself, "How do you want to feel instead?" You can use the confidence Key that we have been using in this section or you can create another positive feeling Key. In any case, stack it and make it nice and strong and test it.

Now, sitting in the audience of your movie theater and firing off your positive Key, holding your positive Key and feeling those positive feelings, see your younger self, on the screen in a "still shot", just before the fearful incident occurred.

THE THREE PLACE WASH

Purpose: To wash away feelings from past traumas, fears, and phobias forever and to learn from them without re-experiencing them.

To let go of the past.

STEPS IN THE THREE PLACE WASH

1. Identify the unwanted state.

2. Establish a positive resource key.

3. From the audience, holding the positive Key, see your younger self in a "still shot" on the screen just prior to the trauma.

4. Float up to the projection booth (Still holding the positive Key).

5. From the projection booth, review the trauma while looking at yourself in the audience watching your younger self on the screen.

6. See the younger self go **beyond** the negative experience and find out what positive and valuable learnings and understanding you received.

7. Float down from the projection booth and become one with audience "self."

8. Go up to the screen and reassure and nurture "younger" self.

9. Actually reach out your arms and slowly re-unite the younger and present "selves."

10. Do a quick future pace.

11. Test by thinking of the negative situation or trauma and notice the change in your feelings.

12. Do an ecological check. That is, imagine a situation in the future when it would be appropriate to feel the negative feelings.

13. Watch for the "Deli Signs!"

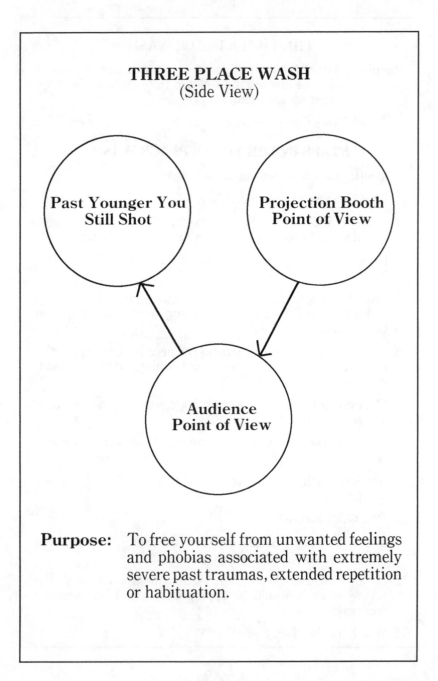

THREE PLACE WASH
(Side View)

Past Younger You
Still Shot

Projection Booth
Point of View

Audience
Point of View

Purpose: To free yourself from unwanted feelings and phobias associated with extremely severe past traumas, extended repetition or habituation.

For example, imagine yourself sitting in the audience, feeling your positive feelings, holding your positive Key and from the audience's point of view you are looking at a still shot of the younger you on the movie screen, just before the traumatic, fearful experience began to occur. In other words, that younger you is feeling okay, the bad experience has not yet happened.

Still holding your positive resource key, mentally float out of your body that's sitting in the audience. Leave your body in the chair and float back and up to the projection booth of the movie theater.

You are now sitting in the projection booth, holding your positive resource Key, feeling solid comfort, feeling in control, feeling positive and confident. From the projection booth you are watching yourself sitting in the audience, looking at the younger you in the still shot on the movie screen.

From the projection booth, feeling solid comfort, watch yourself in the audience, watching the third you on the screen. So, from the projection booth, you are focusing on the back of the head of the "you" in the audience, as the audience you watches the younger you on the screen.

Now turn on the movie and run the scene and let the younger you on the screen go through the fearful scene, the trauma, or that terrible experience and at the same time hold your positive solid comfort Key, feeling solid comfort, staying in the projection booth, looking only at the "you" in the audience.

Run the scene until it is over; until the scene has gone beyond the incident. The younger you has survived the horrible experience and is alright. Great.

Now, still holding your positive resource Key, still feeling solid comfort, run the scene backwards. Then run it forward at high speed. Run it backwards again, even faster. Good. Now turn it upside down and run the scene upside down, forward and then upside down and backward. Take as much time as you need.

Turn the picture to black and white and run the same scene forward and then backward all the while staying in the projection booth holding your positive, solid comfort resource Key.

Then run the scene of the younger you going through that traumatic experience until the horrible experience is over. The episode is finished and you see the younger you beyond the scene and the younger you on the screen has survived.

Now, imagine yourself floating out of the projection booth, still holding your Key, still feeling the solid comfort and float down and enter your body that's sitting in the audience.

Now sitting in the audience, review what happened in that terrible experience, look at that traumatic experience and find some learnings, or understandings that may be of value for you right now. Perhaps there is something you would have liked to have changed. Perhaps you know you have more understanding now or more choices about that experience. Maybe you can see a positive lesson learned. In other words, find one or two things of value you learned from that experience.

Now, mentally get up out of your seat in the audience, still holding the positive Key, walk up to the movie screen and reassure the younger you on the screen that you are from the future and that you survived, you made it and you now have some new learnings, some new understandings and everything is okay.

Perhaps giving the younger you some love, some caring and assurance that the younger you may have needed or now needs. Perhaps an "I love you. Everything is okay. You made it!" Take as much time as you need for this.

When you can see and know the younger you on the screen is truly assured and is feeling good, and that it's over, once and for all, then let go of your Key and actually hold out your arms. Literally, put the book down and hold out your arms right now. Reach out to the younger you and put your arms around the younger you and slowly, gradually pull the younger you inside your body.

You have now reintegrated the younger you into the present you. Let that settle for a moment.

Now, fire off your resource Key again. See yourself in the future, having another experience that is similar to the traumatic experience. However, this time holding your Key, see yourself reacting in a new and different way. See yourself, and feel yourself acting the way that you would like to have felt, the way you'd like to have acted using all of the new resources that you have learned, the positive feelings you have now at a deep level. Keep holding your Key. Good. Now let go of your Key, and go into a neutral state.

Let's test your results. This time don't fire off your Key. Simply think of the situation that just a few minutes ago gave you those negative feelings and notice the difference. If you scaled your original negative feelings on the pre test, you can go back and on the post test scale see how the negative feelings have been reduced.

Do an ecological check now to protect yourself in the future.

If you find that the negative feelings have not been reduced as much as you would like, simply make your positive resource Key stronger and repeat the three place wash activity.

You can also use the future pacing process to deepen the programming.

Now, can you think of a time in the past when the

three place wash would have been valuable to you? Can you imagine a time in the future when this process might be of value to you?

SPECIAL CONSIDERATIONS TO WATCH FOR WHEN DOING THE "THREE PLACE WASH"

When you are doing the three place wash you might find yourself starting to feel fearful or start feeling the feelings you're washing away. If you start getting those negative feelings, that means you are being pulled back into the negative pictures and it is because you are being drawn into the movie.

If that begins to occur, stop the activity. Just back off, take yourself out of the movie, go back into the projection booth. Re-stack the Key to make it stronger with more solid comfort. Then you can, again, manipulate the traumatic scene from the projection booth any way you want.

I had you run it forwards and backwards slowly and then very rapidly, then upside down forwards and upside down backwards, then in black and white forwards and backwards.

You can also run it very, very slowly, like slow motion so it takes minutes to go through the scene. You can chop up the movie into little pieces or frames like a deck of cards and stuff all those shuffled pieces into the projector and run the movie like you're dealing out the cards. The more you can manipulate the scene in different ways, the deeper the programming will be and better the results.

Remember, you don't have to recall the initial experience. You don't have to remember the "cause" of the fear or unwanted feeling. It is enough to remember any situation in the past that gave you those fearful, unwanted feelings. With those more recently known memories, the three place wash will work just as well. And if you have difficulty seeing a clear, complete mental picture, that's okay. Your unconscious will fill in the gaps.

NEUTRAL STATES AND THE BAIL OUT "KEY"

If you are using the three place wash to wash away a severe phobia or extreme negative feelings from a traumatic situation such as a rape, or psychological or physical abuse, it is often a good idea to set up a *bail out* procedure before you do the three place wash. Why? Because sometimes in the case of a very strong fear or trauma, it is difficult to remain in the projection booth.

You can get pulled into the movie and start to feel more negative feelings than you want. As I mentioned before, if that happens, you want to be able to bail out or stop the three place wash quickly.

One way to do this is to create a strong relaxed, calm bail out Key before you do the three place wash. Then, if at anytime, you begin to feel more of the negative feelings than you want, you can fire off the calm, relaxed bail out Key and that will trigger calm relaxed feelings.

You can refer to the page entitled "Creating a Neutral State". These techniques are also good to use to change any feeling at any time or any where.

Another way to get out of the negative feelings is to change what you are doing. Do something different. In other words, get up, move around the room. Think of something else. Get a glass of water or focus your attention outside of your mind into the outside world.

It's best to move from the spot you were sitting or standing because that spot will have become a Key.

CREATING A NEUTRAL STATE
(The Bail Out Procedure)

PURPOSE: To get into a Neutral State and focus outside yourself.

1. Change what you are doing

2. Focus outside your mind into here and now

3. Change your position in room

4. Think of something else

5. Use diaphragmatic breathing

6. Establish a calm, relaxed, and alert Key prior to any activity

---

You can also use deep, diaphragmatic breathing.

You might want to have someone else to do the three place wash with you so they can watch and notice if you happen to get too deeply drawn into the negative feelings. They can, then, bring you out of the experience quickly by shaking you or by saying, "okay, stop the process!" or by using a bail out Key that you have set up with them earlier.

MAKING THE RESULTS OF THE "WASH" EVER STRONGER

You may want to deepen the programming of either the two or three place wash. If you do, an excellent way is to complete the wash and then imagine the younger you going through the traumatic event again. However, this time have the younger you acting the way you would like to have acted, acting with more confidence and assurance, for example, or with fuller resources.

This time, see yourself feeling more positive and more confident instead of fearful. This way you can more deeply change your personal history by reexperiencing the traumatic event with new, positive, confident resources. This will give you even more and stronger choices in the future.

UNBELIEVABLE POSITIVE RESULTS

I have seen unbelievable positive changes in people's lives. Changes that have resulted from washing away fears and other negative feelings associated with past events using the wash.

There is nothing quite as dramatic or quite as touching as seeing a person's life change after they have released themselves from fear or from negative emotions or unwanted habits that have literally held them prisoner.

The changes are so pervasive and profound, they seem to effect every area of their lives. Their self-image improves, their feelings of confidence about themselves spill over into all areas of their lives. Some find their physical and emotional health improves.

The loud, booming negative self-talk has quieted down and have been replaced with warm, loving and confident inner voices. The big, overwhelming picture thoughts have all been reduced to smaller manageable sizes. Positive feelings have made goals appear to be within reach. Faith in a bright, happy future is now a way of life.

All report having more energy and an increased feeling of aliveness. Some people change their attitudes about their jobs, some find better jobs. Some people change how they are living and some where they are living.

Others find their relationships with their loved ones, as well as their business associates, change dramatically. Many find themselves beginning to get more involved in the community and in activities and hobbies they were never able to before. When fear is lifted, a person's thinking and decision-making abilities become sharper and more focused.

Many become more intuitive, more psychic, others become more spiritual.

All are much more interested in planning for the future, in creating goals and taking the steps necessary to achieve those dreams. Washing away fear and eliminating the negative Keys puts more zest, more flavor and more warmth into life.

Life is again filled with more curiosity and wonder. When you begin to use the techniques such as, the Keying process, collapsing Keys, the two and three place wash, and Future pacing you will find that you can have more control over your feelings. You can have more control over your emotions. You will find yourself growing and blooming like a flower in curious and amazing ways you never even imagined.

And as you begin to change, you can use the techniques and the learnings to effect those around you, too. It is especially heartbreaking to see your children or your loved ones become victims of fear and victims of negative Keys they may know nothing about.

However, it is especially satisfying, heartwarming and joyful to be able to use these processes with them, to teach these processes to those around you and allow them to share the changes and the growth and the power that you are experiencing.

GENERALIZING AND FUTURE PROGRAMMING

At this time please turn to the page called "Generalizing and Future Programming" that was discussed earlier.

This written exercise is to future pace the techniques and deepen the understandings that you have learned. They will then be more deeply programmed into your unconscious and be more automatically available to you in the future.

With the information that you've just read or with the activities you've just completed and with the new resources you've just acquired, list three occasions in the past when the learnings and understanding would have been valuable to you. After you have listed the past occasions, remember these situations. One at a time, starting with the most recent situation, write a brief scenario "as if" you had had the new resources you've just learned, and "as if" you are there.

Describe what you would have seen, heard, felt, smelled, tasted, using the new learnings. Start at the beginning of the scenes and go a little beyond the end.

After that, think of three situations in the future when these new techniques, learnings and understandings will be of value to you. Make the first in the near future, within a day or so. The second, later in time; a week to a month in the future. And the third, the farthest from now — perhaps six, nine or twelve months from now. After you have written those down, think of those situations one at a time.

Start with number one and write down what you would see, hear, feel, smell and taste, emotionally feel and do, "as if" you were already there now. Start at the beginning and go beyond the end of each scene. Seeing yourself in the future, using those new techniques, feeling and acting in the positive, powerful ways you want. You have now actively programmed your brain and body to make these resources available to you whenever and wherever you need and want them.

YOU ARE A "KEY"

And remember, *you* are a Key. *You* are a Key to everyone around you. You are a Key to those you love, a Key to those with whom you do business.

What kind of a Key are you? What kind of a Key have you been, positive or negative? What kind of Key do you want to be?

With the knowledge you have gained you now have the power to be a positive Key for everyone in your life and to have everyone in your life, if you choose, to be a positive Key for you.

You have the power to choose the way you want to feel and to choose the way you want to be with anyone. You have the power to choose to be the way you want to be in any situation.

Now to get full value from your program and to make your Keys to more personal power a permanent and natural part of you, you will want to practice these techniques and to actively change those parts of you that you want to change or on which you want to improve.

SUMMARY

You have just learned the extremely powerful techniques of how to control your feelings, wash away fear and eliminate negative feelings association with your past.

You have learned to program in positive feelings of power, confidence, motivation, and resourcefulness, how to expand your comfort zone.

These are all the tools you need to control the principal element of the three keys to more personal power. Controlling your feelings. You now have the tools to control the feel part of the think-feel-do-have success formula.

Let's now look at how these tools can and have been used to increase prosperity, better relationships, better health and peace of mind.

CHAPTER VII.

THE POWER OF POSITIVE FEELINGS FOR BETTER HEALTH, INCREASED PROSPERITY, LOVE AND PEACE OF MIND

SPORTS — DIETS — RELATIONSHIPS — ABUNDANCE

In this section let's look at some examples of how the Keying technique and the power of positive feelings, specifically, has been used in areas as diverse as happiness, health, love and relationships, and financial riches.

A great sage once said that to be successful, prayer is to be practiced like a deserving child talking to a loving mother. A child, who approaches the request knowing he is unconditionally accepted, does so with confidence. The appeal is never constrained with that frame of mind.

Approach life, not as a beggar, but rather with trust. Be clearly focused on your goal yet, let it be lightly held. Practice constructive action with relaxed attention and with a playful frame of mind, and your dreams will materialize.

Let's look at these ideas a little more closely. From them I have isolated five steps to any successful endeavor.

Many sports professionals practice these powerful attitudes, not only in thought, but also in action. Research sponsored by the United States Government on how to teach people to better their Extra Sensory Perception ability, found the identical feelings were required for increased psychic success.

These five steps for any successful endeavor have been and are taught and used by the samurai warrior. The practitioners of the Ninja and their secret form of martial arts, studied these steps until they became automatic. Successful people in all walks of life consciously or unconsciously practice these feelings and attitudes also.

Once these feelings and attitudes are identified, Keying can then be used to more easily make them yours.

FIVE STEP TO SUCCESS

One.   Clearly focused goals lightly held.

Two.   Move with constructive action.

Three.   Maintain relaxed attention.

Four.   Hold a playful frame of mind.

Five.   Persist with a faith in a Higher Power.

Number one, *clearly focused goals* lightly held means to be outcome oriented. Not trying too hard. Therefore creating little resistance and increasing flexibility.

Number two, move with *constructive action*, allows you to move with no lost motion. Every action has a purpose; wasting no thoughts, feelings or actions.

Maintaining action with *relaxed attention* as in number three, gives you the ability to move forward in a more assured way. To go ahead attending to priorities with faith and confidence.

Number four is not only effective but also fun. Holding a *playful frame of mind* creates an attitude of playfulness and fun. It increases creativity and generates more flexibility. It also helps to keep us aware of the Divine truth that life is only a game. And, we are little children in big bodies trying to figure it all out. We then can more easily stay on top of things and have the panoramic vision needed to have *fun* and succeed.

Persisting with a faith in a Higher Power, number five. This attitude also helps us see the big picture and the Divine plan and pattern in nature's schema. It keeps us humble. When we are humble, we are teachable. And only when we are teachable can we more readily see what the next step is to be.

With faith we can act with abandon — the attitude of the warrior. The frame of mind of the winner!

SPORTS

One 19 year old man was becoming a *tennis* pro when he hit a snag in his playing. He would reach a certain score and "choke". No matter how hard he tried he would freeze whenever the score would reach three games to three. No matter how or when that happened he would become tense and blow it. After teaching him the Keying process, he broke through his comfort zone and overcame his problem.

He would slap his left leg in the same place as his Key. He practiced this and future paced it until it became unconscious. Then his body memories took over. He's now a professional and can be seen on the professional tennis circuit.

Olympic professionals use the Keying process all the time. It was reported that Carl Lewis, the champion 500 meter runner, would get "as if" feelings before every race by remembering other races he had won. Then while holding those feelings he would see himself having already won. He would go beyond his goal. He would see himself at home telling his friends and relative how he had won the race he was about to run! What a beautiful way to get those peak performance feelings.

Winning pitcher Orel Hershiser, of the Los Angeles Dodgers, during the 1988 World Series playoffs used hymns as Keys to keep him calm when he was not out there on the pitcher's mound. He would hum the hymn in his head which kept him from worrying about the next inning.

Internationally known ski champion, John Keely, when rushing down the ski slopes used phrases from the Bible to keep focused.

Master performers. Warriors to be emulated for sure!

HAPPINESS AND OVERCOMING FEAR

I'll never forget, the first time I was on the *Merv Griffin Show*. Here I am, the fear expert of the world. And here I am, sitting back in the Celebrity Room, the green room, with Robert Foxworth from *Falcon Crest* and Loretta Swift from MASH.

They are sitting there sipping apple juice like Cool Hand Lukes. And I'm looking at them and I'm getting stiff sitting on the edge of my chair. Now being a fear expert I can recognize terror. And that was terror!

I thought, "Oh no!" So I reach over and fire off my Key and it wasn't strong enough. So I did what I say in my cassette albums, "If what you do doesn't work, do something different. And if that do something different doesn't work, then boogie!"

So I stood up and I started jiggling around and shaking the toxins out of my body to release all that tied up energy in there.

Then, I thought of a time when I was showing off in front of Mom. I remembered a time when I had secretly been practicing some cartwheels, hand springs and a flip or two in the back yard. After I got pretty good, I called Mom out to see my show. She's feeling real proud, now, and I'm feeling real proud. And when I got those good, proud show off feelings, I stacked them right on my Key.

I did that two or three times and Keyed them in. I stacked those show off feelings, and when they opened the curtains to let me go out on the stage to be introduced to Merv and the audience, I fired off the show off Key. I went out there, and like Donna Summers says, "When you got it, flaunt it!" I really didn't do that. I actually went out and did quite well.

That's one way to take care of fear and to be happy.

Another great story about Keying in happiness is about a middle aged women who suffered from agoraphobia. She couldn't leave her house for fear of having a panic attack. She had tried everything, but nothing seemed to work. That is until she remembered a wonderful, happy time when she was with her father and the sweet aroma of roses was all around them. She then went to the gift shop and bought potpourri scented with the smell of sweet roses. Her Key was the fragrance of roses! With this Key, she has successfully overcome her agoraphobia and has been conducting a successful boutique business ever since.

You might want to refer in your Appendices to the "Daily Affirmation". These are the frames of mind that the successful and happy hold when they approach their world.

HEALTH

One of my favorite, favorite students is a retired veterinarian by the name of Rollins. Rollins was 70 years old and he was losing his memory. Or, I should say, he thought he was losing his memory. After only one week of listening to the cassette album "Through The Briar Patch", and learning how to use the Key he was cured.

After one week, he was talking to me and he said, "You know what Dr. Dossey? A miracle has occurred. Not only did I get my memory back but my golf got better, and my tennis got better. And, you know what? Even my relationship with my wife got better!"

Then, three months later he wrote me a letter saying, "Dr. Dossey, I recently went to my eye doctor for my regular check up and I had to get new glasses. My eyes got better. My vision got better. Thank you very much."

Let's take a look at what happened to Rollins. When he was developing his Key, he would remember times in the past when he was younger. When he was child like. When he had more energy. Remember, the mind and body are inseparable and they never forget. So, what happened was he reactivated the young physiology in his body/mind. That gave him more energy and got his memory back.

Another thing that has been done in terms of bettering health is the lowering of high blood pressure and the heart rate. We've done it in 30 minutes. You can do it by simply remembering times when you didn't have hypertension, times when your blood pressure was low and you were more relaxed. When the low blood pressure begins to be accessed in the body, Key it in.

A 38 year old woman had a harrowing experience in the hospital. She had a Caesarean section and the doctors were yelling at each other as she was going under the anesthetic. As a result, she had high blood pressure every time she would go near a doctor's office. The doctor's office and hospitals became negative Keys. Keys that triggered off all the horrible feelings about the harrowing birth that would send her blood pressure up.

So, every time she would go to the doctor's office the doctor would take her blood pressure and it would be high. The doctor insisted she take certain pills or she would die. She didn't want to take the pills, so she decided she would go to another doctor.

The next doctor told her the same thing, "Your blood pressure is going to kill you if you don't take this medication."

She finally came to the Phobia Institute. I had her remember times in her life prior to the hospital experience. As she did that, I notice a new calmness on her face. Then she Keyed those calm, relaxed feelings in. After 20 or 30 minutes, I took her blood pressure and it was normal. Lowering blood pressure and heart rate will lengthen your life.

Migraine headaches and backaches have now become a thing of the past for those who have used the Keying process in the same way as this woman did for lowering her blood pressure.

Reactivating or increasing the activity of the immune system itself can now be done with the use of the Keying technique. Remember, when you are in negative thinking, when you are in fear, depression, or in any negative feeling, the activation of the immune system slows down. That means you have fewer white blood corpuscles in the blood stream. That means you are more susceptible to viruses, germs and disease. Coronary disease, and even cancer, has now been linked to a stress and fear based process.

The endorphins, nature's analgesic, morphine-like pain killers which we create in our bodies, can now increased by using the Key and the Keying process, by going back and reactivating the child like feelings.

When we were little kids the immune system in most of us was operating at full bore. We had more energy, we were healthy. We could even eat dirt. Remember when you went around eating mud pies? Well, I did anyway. Our immune systems were active and well. And now, with the proper use of the Keys, there is the possibility of attaining and maintaining better health.

DIETS

Obsessive or compulsive overeating is invariably due to not dealing with unwanted feelings. These feelings are often not even known by the over eater. Sometimes they are.

The first step is for the over eater to become aware of the feelings they are trying to stuff down. Once that has been accomplished, Keying then becomes the obvious next step.

A middle aged man who couldn't control his eating, was grossly overweight and had tried every diet known. He tried powders and failed. He attempted protein and failed. He tried fruit only and that didn't work. He tried them all. Then he tried Keying.

He began by slowing down before he ate anything. He learned to ask about his feelings. Once he could identify real feeling, such as hunger, anger, tired, lonely, etc., he would ask the next operative question. What did he want to feel instead? And then he proceeded through the Keying technique. In only three weeks he had a handle on the unwanted feelings and began to automatically lose weight. Now he eats what he wants and doesn't have to worry about gaining weight any more.

ABUNDANCE

Andra, a young 28 year old producer/writer, was horribly depressed. She was really down in the dumps. Her husband had left her and their two children. She had lost all of her money. She was being kicked out of her home. She needed some money to finish a project she was working on. And to top it all off, her mother's car had fallen apart.

We began Keying in times when she had money. When she was prosperous. We even had her think of people who had even more money than she had ever had. That created the "as if" physiology. She thought of those rich people and stepped into their bodies and Keyed it in. After she got those abundant "as if" feelings, she zoomed out of the office, flying.

Two weeks later, Andra came back and she had this look on her face that looked like the cat had just sucked up the milk. And I said, "My goodness, my goodness Andra. What has happened to you? How is it you are feeling so good?" She said, "Dr. Dossey you wont believe it. A miracle of miracles. After we Keyed in those abundant feelings, I went on TIC TAC DO and won $37,000! And guess what one of the prizes was? That's right a car!"

What I believe was happening with Andra was that the self fulfilling prophesy or the Deli Sign phenomenon was working. It was a treatment that began to set up the trajectory that led to prosperity. Then, the subconscious mind with the superconscious mind (the Cosmic Consciousness or God, whatever you choose to call it) began to allow her to see the Deli Signs that were already there.

LOVE AND LOVING RELATIONSHIPS

When discussing love, I'm not only talking about the love as in romantic love like Rollins had. But, I'm also talking about the love of family. I'm talking about the love of children. I'm talking about the love of our parents and our friends.

I'm also talking about the love of the spirit of life, and of life itself. I'm talking about all those kinds of love. And you can have any or all of those kinds of love.

If you do want romance, if you do want a romantic relationships, you can remember times when you were loving and in love. I'm not talking about wishful thinking here. I mean real "as if" feelings of love. And then Key those feelings in. The Deli Signs will begin to pop up before your very eyes.

Here's a formula I like very much when it comes to love and loving relationships. Naome Rhodes, a well known motivational speaker, said, "We are always building memories." Think of that. We are always building memories. We are a Key ourselves. We're a Key! And if we are out in the world talking about negative things, if we're out there talking depressing things, or talking about tight economies, guess how our friends and associates are going to feel when they think of us. Because we are each a Key.

I'm sure everyone of us has that one person in our life, who, if they walked into the room right now would cause us to go "Oh no, no. no!" Because they are a negative Key and may not even know it.

We're always building memories. We're either building up our relationships or we're tearing them down. There is no such thing as a static relationship. A still river begins to dry up.

Dr. Harry Douglas Smith, one of my mentors, said, "Think as if your life depends upon it because it does." I'd like to add to that, "Think and *feel* and act "as if" your life depends upon it because it does!"

So, if you want love, simply be loveable and be loving. Then you'll be able to Key in all those wonderful feelings. You will be a love Key for the rest of the world.

Now let's find out how and why smiling is the most powerful Key in the universe.

CHAPTER VIII.

"SMILE POWER' — THE ULTIMATE "KEY" TO HAPPINESS!

We have now come to one of my favorite findings and a most curious and interesting thing about Keys and Keying.

As I was doing research at the Phobia Institute, I noticed that people would look like they were smiling, or would have pleasant looking expressions on their faces when they were Keying in pleasant feelings. So, I arbitrarily had my patients begin faking a smile when staking a Key, thinking it might help in strengthening the Key. I didn't really know what I was doing until the Keying process was written up in *Omni Magazine* not too long ago. The article was about how we were using the revolutionary Keying technique to quickly wash away fears and phobias.

In the same section, there was a report of some research being done at Drake University by a Dr. James Laird. Dr. Laird would have people read grim, depressing editorials and then, he would have the people read some comics by Woody Allen.

Then he would have the people fake a smile. When they would fake a smile, an interesting thing happened. When faking a smile, they could remember more of the funny stories. When he had them fake a frown or a grimace, however, they could remember more of the depressing editorials than they could the comics.

Dr. Laird then had the patients fake a smile and think of something relatively innocuous, for most, like a car. This time, while faking a smile, the people would remember happy incidents relating to cars. But, when the faked a frown they would recall unhappy or stressful occasions. Like wiping out dad's car.

He was using this *smile power* to interrupt the pattern of depression. He also knew that no two feelings could occupy or go through the same neurological track. So, the patients could not stay depressed while faking a smile.

That confirmed what my own research had shown me: the power of a smile, real or fake.

Then, I realized something even more profound. That was, that a smile is really a phylogenetic, positive Key. That is, a smile is an inborn Key. A cross cultural Key.

There is not a culture on this planet where people frown when they are happy or smile when they are sad. A smile is natures inborn, God given positive Key! A Natural Key stronger than any Key we could create by squeezing our wrists.

Now I'm suggesting to all of my patients, and to you, to smile or fake a smile to create positive resource feelings, and to make any Key stronger. Smiling is a Key.

Psychologists did further research with polygraphs in which professional actors and actresses would fake certain emotions. After faking an emotion, like fear, their bodies would begin to respond physiologically "as if" they had the fear! Their bodies and the polygraphs didn't know the difference between real and imagined fear.

The same results were found with other feelings like happiness and sadness. The bodies didn't know the difference between real and faked feelings!

You can use a smile when stacking a positive Key, and it will make the Key even stronger. Or you can use the smile as the Key itself.

Since research has found smiling is already a positive, happy Key, a Key you were born with, why not smile when you are not happy and you will become happy! And if you smile when you feel bad, you will feel better. Smiling is a positive physical Key. The homey sayings like, "Put on a happy face.", "Smile and the world smiles with you." and "Let a smile be your umbrella" are sound scientific prescriptions!

Try it. Just fake a smile right now. Give it some time. You may feel a little funny at first, maybe a little embarrassed.

But if you give it a few seconds or even a few seconds more, you will find that those positive, happy feelings begin to fill your body. Make a great big ear to ear smile. Now, notice how you begin to feel.

So smile real big right now and you can take your Smile Power with you as you face life's challenging opportunities.

Smile Power is the ultimate Key to happiness!

FINAL FAREWELL — ONE FINAL NOTE TO GUARANTEE YOUR SUCCESS

One final note. You now have in your hands access to a regular, ongoing source of strength and guidance with positive and practical suggestions to help you effectively face life's challenging opportunities. Share your new learnings with your loved one, friends and associates. Remember, you are always building memories.

Take your new learnings into the world. Make the world your experimental laboratory in which you can learn, stretch, and grow for the rest of your life. *You can* make a difference. *You can* make the world a better place in which to live.

With the information in this book, and Keying specifically, commit yourself to the excitement of risk taking.

Set your goals high, but not so they prevent you from trying and doing the best you can. Instead of pretending to be a perfectionist, be content that you are making progress. The important thing is to be focused and moving forward. Perfectionism is only the result of false pride and an excuse to save face. Be willing to make mistakes and stumble. The Universe guides the person who is stumbling forward.

Be not so interested in what you are as in what you are becoming. We are all on the way, not at the goal. And, we will be on the path as long as we live. No one has ever "arrived".

An unknown author wrote:

The Risk of Being Free

To laugh is to risk appearing the fool.

To weep is to risk appearing sentimental.

To reach out for another is to risk involvement.

To expose feelings is to risk exposing your true self.

To place your ideas, your dreams, before the crowd is to risk their loss.

To love is to risk not being loved in return.

To live is to risk dying.

To hope is to risk despair.

To try is to risk failure.

But risks must be taken because the greatest hazard in life is to risk nothing. The person who risks nothing does nothing, has nothing, is nothing. He may avoid suffering and sorrow, but he simply cannot learn, feel change, grow, love . . . Live. Chained by his certitudes, he is a slave; he has forfeited freedom. Only a person who risks is free.

Thank you and have a joyful journey!

APPENDICES
I, II, and III

APPENDIX I.

DR. DOSSEY'S
FEAR AND PHOBIA FINDER

PURPOSE:

1. To assist you in identifying and locating from over 250 fears and phobias, to the most troublesome unwanted habits, blocks and barriers.

2. To give you a list of step-by-step Change Strategies in a cookbook approach to handle these Challenging Opportunities in the deepest, most profound, pervasive and lasting way.

HOW TO USE YOUR FEAR AND
PHOBIA FINDER

1. Simply go though the list, locate and identify your Challenging Opportunity.

2. Begin applying the list of Change Strategies starting at the top of your "Levels of Change Pyramid". (See list, "Levels of Change Pyramid")

Use this Pyramid as a guide to overcoming thoughts and feelings, habits or behaviors that may be in your way and keeping you from your various goals. As you go from the top to the all pervasive bottom of the Pyramid, each level increases the probability of altering the physiology (body memories) more predictably and permanently. Thus, adding more choices and possibilities in attaining your desired outcomes.

All of the activities can be used to interrupt any unwanted patterns. If the first one you try doesn't work, do something different and go deeper into the Levels of Change Pyramid until you find one that does.

LEVELS OF CHANGE PYRAMID

1. Do something different - Interrupt the pattern by:

   a. Physically changing positions, move around or rehearse doing something different; or

   b. Mentally re-framing situation from a problem to a challenging opportunity, holding a different winning assumption or point of view.

2. Use Five Dimensional Goal Setting — especially the Outcome Frame.

3. Future Pacing — Focusing Beyond situation to desired outcome.

4. Keying Process.

5. Collapsing Keys for deleting negative habits and adding positive choices.

6. Changing Personal History. Two and Three Place Wash.

7. Future Pace with Key.

8. Smile Power

9. Prayer — Faith — Turn it over.

*Note: Some things are better handled by calling a professional who is an expert. This program is to be used as an adjunct to professional help.

FEAR AND PHOBIA FINDER

WHAT IS PHOBIA

The classical definition of a Phobic Disorder is, ". . . irrational, persistent fear of or an excessive avoidance of a specific object, some particular activity or situation."

The American Psychiatric Association subdivides Phobic Disorders into three types:

1. *Agoraphobia*: fear of open spaces, the most common and severe of phobias.

2. *Social Phobia*: fear of embarrassment or ridicule in social situations.

3. *Simple Phobia*: fear of specific discreet objects, situations or activities.

All three types can be with or without panic attacks.

The following is a partial list of these three subdivisions:

AGORAPHOBIA: Fear of . . . .

Crowded spaces:
  Stores
  Elevators
  Public transportation
  Theaters
  Churches & Synagogues

Leaving familiar settings,
Leaving home

Leaving place of business

Promotions
Flying
Change of job
Traveling in

automobiles

Moving
Change of neighborhood
Standing in line

Driving on freeways
Traveling on trains,
buses, boats, etc.

Crossing streets
Being alone
Losing a loved one

SOCIAL PHOBIA: Fear of . . .

Ridicule
Losing Face
Blushing
Embarrassment
Delegating authority
Eating in public alone
Assuming responsibility

Talking to superiors
Job security
Social functions
Failure
Financial security
Public speaking
Success
Writing for publications

SIMPLE PHOBIA: Fear of . . .

Air	Aerophobia
Animals	Zoophobia
Auroral lights	Auroraphobia
Bacteria	Bacteriophobia
	Microbiophobia
Beards	Pogonophobia
Bees	Apiphobia
	Melissephobia
Being afraid	Phobophobia
Being alone	Agoraphobia
	Monophobia
	Eremophobia
Being beaten	Rhobdophobia
Being bound	Merinthophobia
Being buried alive	Taphophcbia
Being dirty	Automysophobia
Being found out as Imposter	Imponereophobia
Being egotistical	Autophobia
Being scratched	Amychophobia
Being stared at	Scopophobia
Birds	Ornithophobia
Blood	Hematophobia
Blushing	Ereuthophobia
Books	Bibliophobia
Cancer	Cancerophobia
	Carcinomatophobia
Cats	Gatophobia
Certain name	Onomatophobia
Change, moving	Tropophobia
Chickens	Alektorophobia
Childbirth	Tocophobia
Children	Pediophobia
China	Sinophobia
Choking	Pnigophobia
Cholera	Cholerophobia
Churches	Ecclestaphobia
Clouds	Nephophobia
Cold	Psychrophobia
	Frigophobia
Colors	Chromatophobia

Computers	Technophobia
	Computophobia
Corpse	Neerophobia
Crossing a bridge	Gephyrophobia
Crowds	Ochilophobia
Crystals	Crystallophobia
Dampness	Hygrophobia
Dawn	Eosophobia
Daylight	Phengophobia
Death	Necrophophobia
Decision-making	Decidophobia
Deformity	Dysmorphophobia
Demons, devils	Demonophobia
Depth	Bathophobia
Dirt	Mysophobia
	Rhypophobia
Disease	Nosophobia
	Pathophobia
Disorder	Ataxiophobia
Dogs	Cynophobia
Dolls	Pediophobia
Draught	Anemophobia
Dreams	Oneirophobia
Drink	Potophobia
Drinking	Dipsophobia
Driving on expressway	Dronophobia
Drugs	Pharmacophobia
Duration	Chronophobia
Dust	Amathophobia
Earthquakes	Seismosophobia
	Seismophobia
Electricity	Electrophobia
Elevated places, heights	Acropbobia
Empty rooms	Kenophobia
Enclosed space	Claustrophobia
England and things English	Anglophobia
Everything	Panophobia
	Panphobia
Eyes	Ommatophobia
Faces	Coprophobia
Failure	Kakorraphiaphobia

Fatigue	Ponopholia
Fear	Phobopbia
Feathers	Preronophobia
Fire	Pyrophobia
Fish	Iclathyophobia
Flashes	Selaphobia
Flogging	Mastigophobia
Flood	Anthophobia
Flowers	Anthophobia
Flute	Anlophobia
Flying	Aerophobia
Fog	Homichlophobia
Food	Shophobia
	Cibophobia
Foreigners	Zenophobia
	Xenophobia
France and things French	Gallophobia
Freedom	Eleutherophobia
Friday the 13th.	Paraskavedekatriaphobia
Fur	Doraphobia
Germany and things German	Germanophobia
Germs	Spermophobia
Ghosts	Phasmophobia
Glass	Crystallophobia
	Hyalophobia
God	Theophobia
Going to bed	Clinophobia
Grave	Taphophobia
Gravity	Barophobia
Hair	Chaetophobia
Halloween	Shamhainophobia
Heart disease	Cardiophobia
Heat	Thermophobia
Heaven	Ouranophobia
Heights	Acrophobia
Heredity	Patroiophobia
Home surroundings	Ecophobia
	Oikophobia
Home	Donatophobia
Horses	Hippophobia
Human beings	Anthropophobia

Ice, frost	Cryophobia
Ideas	Ideophobia
Illness	Nosomaphobia
Imperfection	Atelophobia
Indecisiveness	Decidophobia
Infection	Mysophobia
	Molysmophobia
Infinity	Apeirophobia
Inoculation, injections	Trypanophobia
Insanity	Lyssophobia
	Maniaphobia
Insects	Entomophobia
Itching	Acarohobia
	Scabiophobia
Jealousy	Zelophobia
Justice	Dikephobia
Knees	Genuphobia
Lakes	Linanophobia
Leprosy	Lerophobia
Lice	Pediculophobia
Light	Photophobia
	Phengophobia
Lightning	Astrapophobia
	Keraunophobia
Love	Amoraphobia
Machinery	Mechanophobia
Making false statements	Mythophobia
Many things	Polyphobia
Marriage	Gamophobia
Meat	Carnophobia
Men	Andropbobia
Metals	Metallophobia
Meteors	Meterophobia
Mice	Musophobia
Microbes	Bacilliphobia
Mind	Psychophobia
Mirrors	Eisopnophobia
Missiles	Ballistophobia
Moisture	Hygrophobia
Money	Chrometophobia
Monstrosities	Teratophobia

Motion	Kinesophobia
Nakedness	Gymnophobia
Names	Nomatophobia
Needles and pins	Belonophobia
Neglect of duty	Parlipophobia
Narrowness	Anginaphobia
New	Neophobia
Night	Nyctophobia
Noise or loud talking	Phonophobia
Novelty	Cainophobia
	Neophobia
Ocean	Thalassophobia
Odors	Osmophobia
Odors (body)	Osphresiophobia
Oneself	Autophobia
One thing	Monophobia
Open spaces	Agoraphobia
	Cenophobia
	Kenophobia
Pain	Algophobia
	Odynephobia
Parasites	Parasitophobia
	Pluhariophobia
Peanut Butter sticking	Arachibutyrophobia
to roof of mouth	
People	Anthropophobia
Physical love	Arotophobia
Places	Topophobia
Pleasure	Hedonophobia
Points	Aichurophobia
Poison	Toxiphobia
Poverty	Peniaphobia
Pregnancy	Matensiophobia
Precipices	Cremnophobia
Punishment	Painophobia
Rabies	Lyssophobia
Railways	Siderodromophobia
Rain	Ombrophobia
Responsibility	Hypergiaphobia
Reptiles	Batrachophobia
Ridicule	Katagelophobia

Rivers	Potamophobia
Robbers	Harpaxophobia
Ruin	Atephobia
Russia or things Russian	Russophobia
Rust	Iophobia
Sacred things	Hierophobia
Satan	Satanophobia
School	Scholionophobia
	Didaskaleinophobia
Sea	Thakasophobia
Sea swell	Cymophobia
Sex	Genophobia
Sexual intercourse	Coitophobia
	Cypridophobia
Shadows	Sciophobia
Sharp objects	Belonophobia
Shock	Hormephobia
Sinning	Peccatophobia
Skin	Dermatophobia
Skin diseases	Dermatosiophobia
Sitting idle	Thaasophobia
Skin of animals	Doraphobia
Sleep	Hypnophobia
Slime	Blennophobia
Smell	Olfactophobia
Smothering	Pnigerophobia
Snakes	Ophidiophobia
Snow	Chionophobia
Society	Anthropophobia
Solitude	Eremophobia
Sound	Akousticophobia
Sourness	Acerophobia
Speaking	Halophobia
Speaking aloud	Phonophobia
Speech	Lalophobia
Speed	Tachophobia
Spiders	Arachmophobia
Spirits	Demonophobia
Stagefright or performing	Topophobia
Standing upright	Stasiphobia
Stars	Siderophobia

Stealing	Cleptophobia
Sullenness	Eremophobia
Stings	Cnidophobia
Stooping	Kyphophobia
Strangers	Xenophobia
String	Linonophobia
Sun	Heliophobia
Surgical operations	Ergasiophobia
Swallowing	Phagophobia
Syphilis	Syphilophobia
Taste	Geumatophobia
Technology	Technophobia
Teeth	Odontophobia
Thirteen at table or number 13	Triskaidekaphobia
Thunder	Keraunophobia
	Tonitrophobia
Touching or being touched	Haphephobia
Toxic chemicals in environment	Microchememophobia
Travel	Hodophobia
Trees	Dendrophobia
Trembling	Tremophobia
Tuberculosis	Phihisiophobia
Uncovering the body	Gymnophobia
Vehicles	Amaxophobia
	Ochophobia
Venereal disease	Cypridophobia
	Venerophobia
Void	Kenophobia
Vomiting	Emetophobia
Walking	Basiphobia
	Batophobia
Wasps	Spheksophobia
Water	Hydrophobia
Weakness	Asthenophobia
Wind	Anemophobia
Witches	Wicaphobia
Women	Gynophobia
Words	Logophobia
	Verbophobia

Work	Ergasiophobia
	Ponophobia
Worms	Helminthophobia
Wounds, injury	Traumatophobia
Writing	Graphophobia
Young girls	Parthenophobia

Again, this is only a *partial* listing.

At the Phobia Institute of West Los Angeles, these delineations have been expanded further and defines a phobia as "any behavior or feeling that is unacceptable and uncomfortable resulting from conscious or unconscious pictures of the past or projected pictures of the future . . . or . . . any thoughts or actions that result in debilitating behavior and decreased optimum performance."

Phobic behavior ranges from mild anxiety to the extreme phobic reaction of physiological or physical stress. Some commonplace symptoms of Phobic Disorder can be categorized in three areas: Physiological, Emotional, Social or Work-related.

SOME PHYSIOLOGICAL (OR PHYSICAL) SYMPTOMS OF PHOBIC DISORDERS:

Hypertension
Increased / decreased blood pressure
Increased / decreased heart rate
Temporary blindness
Sweaty palms
Sweating
Hyperventilation
Vertigo Coronary disease
Headaches — backaches
Overeating
Alcohol & Substance abuse
Muscle tightness and/or spasms

Paralyzed limbs
Wry neck
Palpitations
Nausea
Vomiting
Gas Pains
Diarrhea

Respiratory disease
Fainting
Coma

SOME EMOTIONAL SYMPTOMS OF PHOBIC DISORDERS:

Anxiety
Nervousness
Irritability
Worrying
Confusion
Sleeplessness
Depression
Impaired thinking
Nightmares
Hysterics

Uncertainty
Excessive dependency
Hostility
Insomnia
Hypochondriacal behavior
Paranoid reactions
Disorientation
Delusions
Hallucinatory behavior
Panic

SOME SOCIAL OR WORK RELATED
SYMPTOMS OF PHOBIC DISORDERS:

Forgetfulness	Increase in errors
Low productivity	Job performance anxiety
Unconscious sabatoge	Lack of attentiveness
Absenteeism	Boredom
Burn-out	Sexual dysfunction
Communication breakdowns	Divorce
Indecisiveness	Low grades
Alcoholism	Irritability
Substance Abuse	

Children and adolescents also suffer from Phobic Disorders such as "School Phobias".

In fact, phobias in children are so common, that they have been referred to as "childhood neuroses". If you think about it, there are probably very few of us who haven't, at some time in early life, experienced fear of a phobic nature.

Some typical **CHILDHOOD PHOBIAS** include Fear of . . .

Abandonment	The Dark
Leaving parents	Being Lost
Other kids	Animals
Teachers and authority figures	Illness
Ghosts, witches and demons	Operations
Pain	Hurt

Victims of crime, rape victims, and victims of disaster and trauma, are still another segment of our society who experience Phobic Disorders.

There are others who suffer from fears about obesity, alcohol, drugs, smoking, job responsibility, flying and both personal and business security. Most people at some time or other experiences FEAR OF CHANGE! Finally, every human being undergoes some degree of the following:

LIFE CYCLE PHOBIAS: Fear of . . .

Starting school	Losing children
Puberty	Divorce
Getting out of school	Middle age
Going to work	Growing old
Dating	Senility
Getting married	Disease
Having children	Death & Dying

In fact, any sights, sound, memories or thoughts of things or situations which result in negative feelings or undesirable reactions can be considered a Phobia.

However, there is hope now. Once you have identified your Challenging Opportunity, select the appropriate process on your "Level of Change Pyramid" and wash away your unwanted fear or habit.

Have fun and keep your eyes open for the Deli Signs!

APPENDIX II.

DAILY AFFIRMATIONS

AFFIRMATIONS AND PRESUPPOSITIONS TO PERSONAL POWER

The following is a group of ideas, points-of-view or frames of mind from which successful and happy people approached their world. They are philosophical positions happy and successful people hold to be true or assume to be true. Holding these Affirmations or Frame of Mind makes the attainment of success virtually a guarantee.

Use the Affirmations by daily choosing one of these presuppositions that best fits your particular interest. Think about it, ponder and reflect upon it four or five times during the day. This will deepen the programming and make it yours. Do this for 30 days and watch out for the Deli Signs.

AFFIRMATIONS —

1. What I hold to be true is created in my world.

2. If anyone has ever done something, I can do it too. And if no one has ever done it, why not me?

3. Anything is possible to me.

4. I can always have a good day.

5. Everyone is giving it their best and only shot and that includes me.

6. I can never fail. The only way I can fail is if I quit trying.

7. There are no such things as mistakes, problems, or failures. There are only results. And these results are exciting, challenging opportunities to exercise my creativity.

8. What I act like is true, becomes true.

9. My positive self-worth stays constant from birth, I am always a loving, caring, curious and wonderful being and only my behavior changes.

10. I do not have to suffer to grow.

11. It doesn't have to take a long time to grow.

12. I have no broken parts.

13. It's okay to be Powerful.

14. It's okay to think, feel, do and have what I want.

15. I have faith in a Power greater than myself and I know the Unconscious fills in the gaps.

16. I am enough.

17. I have within me all of the resources to achieve anything I desire.

18. All my behavior is controlled by neurological patterns.

19. There is no substitute for my clear sensory awareness.

20. I can only succeed.

21. My aim is to be of value to myself and others and my target is to make a contribution to the world.

22. All of my feelings are okay and are my friends that gave necessary signals. I do not have to act upon them.

23. There is no such thing as a "resistant" or ineffective student. There are only inflexible, ineffective teachers.

24. I do not need to be fixed. Therefore, I continually build upon my strengths. It's not my bad habits that count. It's my good ones.

25. I am a fun oriented and a "happy addict" and I hold a Positive Mental Attitude 51% of the time.

26. I know life is only a game and I am always on the winning side.

27. I love challenges and risk taking.

28. I know it's not the outside world, or people in it, that creates my feelings or actions, but rather it's my reactions to the outside world that creates my experiences.

29. I see the bright side and good in all situations.

30. I can stay on top of the mountain and discern learnings from every experience.

31. I practice forgiveness; especially forgiveness of myself.

32. The more any action taken serves others, the more the chances of successful and satisfying results. It's a direct ratio.

33. I know its best to think and feel as if my life depends upon it, because it does!

34. I'm enough.

35. I won't let yesterday take too much of today's time.

36. COURAGE is having known fears and limitations and doing it anyway.

37. I can only succeed. Going only one-half of the way is always 100% farther than I was.

38. I know misery is always an option.

39. I am like the warrior. With relaxed attention and the courage of wonder and curiosity, I can accomplish anything.

40. I see all "problems" or "barriers" as challenging opportunities.

41. I know happiness is taking action; taking risks.

42. I know happiness and success is guaranteed when I am being thankful, holding a positive attitude, practicing positive prayer, and taking action.

43. I know I am never given more than I can handle.

44. I can accomplish miracles when I accept anxiety as another name for challenge.

45. I realize that every decision is made with insufficient data.

46. I am willing to accept the realization that IT'S ONLY A GAME!

APPENDIX III.

THE PHOBIA INSTITUTE OF WEST LOS ANGELES AND STRESS MANAGEMENT CENTERS OF SOUTHERN CALIFORNIA

We are dedicated to the research and treatment of any malady that besets the human condition. We have incorporated Dr. Dossey's complete "Seven Steps to Personal Growth" Program.

This Seven Step program is the most comprehensive approach that virtually guarantees success in any facet of your life. It enhances Dr. Dossey's Think/feel/do/have motivation and success formula.

1. Refocusing Techniques (Controlling you Mind)

2. Keying (Controlling your Feelings)

3. Multi-Dimensional Goal Setting System (Controlling your Actions)

4. Relaxation Techniques

5. Physical Activity For Fun

6. Power Foods

7. Predictable Communication Strategies

This exciting information can be yours through our new Home Seminar audio cassette programs with Dr. Dossey recorded live.

**CALL OR WRITE TO ORDER CASSETTE
PROGRAMS OR FOR MORE INFORMATION
ABOUT THE INSTITUTE.**

1. DIAGNOSTIC EVALUATIONS
2. TELEPHONE HOME TREATMENT PROGRAM
3. LIVE SEMINARS WITH DR. DOSSEY
4. SPEAKERS BUREAU

NEW HOME SEMINAR
CASSETTE PROGRAMS
with DR. DONALD DOSSEY

THROUGH THE BRIAR PATCH: In this Home Seminar Program you will learn all of the concrete tools to predictably master Dr. Dossey's "Seven Step Personal Growth Program". Controlling your mind, controlling your feelings and controlling your actions. How to let go of the past and create a future you can chart with ease; and how to wash away any fears, phobias or stress. Six hours. $150.00

PREDICTABLE COMMUNICATION STRATEGIES: A program with NEW communication techniques to better personal relationships, sales and business outcome. Excellent for strengthening relationships. Great for trainers, managers, sales, and counseling practitioners. 4 hours $95.00

"KEYING" IN SUCCESS: Teaching his world famous Keying technique, Dr. Dossey explains how to eliminate fear and depressions, better your health, enrich love and increase financial security. One hour 20 min. $15.00

MAKING RESOLUTIONS WORK: After listening to Dr. Dossey being interviewed by radio KBIG's Phil Reed, making New Year's Resolutions work will be easy and fun. 30 Minutes $10.00.

GOAL EFFECTIVENESS TRAINING: A program that teaches you nuts and bolts of manipulating your mind and behavior to more predictably reach your desires. NEW and exciting research findings never before presented to the general public. Learn how to let go of the past and re-route your future. Four hours. $95.00

BOOK — KEYING: THE POWER OF POSITIVE FEELINGS by Donald E. Dossey, Ph.D. $14.95

- - - - - - - - - - - - - - - - - - - -*ORDER FORM*- - - - - - - - - - - - - - - - - - - -

(Please add $2.00 for shipping and handling for book and $5.00 for shipping and handling audio cassette programs. Calif. residents add 6½% sales tax.)

☐ Payment enclosed   Please charge my   ☐ Visa   ☐ MasterCard

Acct. # _____Exp. Date _____

Signature_____

Please send me _____

_____Total Amount $_____

Name_____Tele (_____)_____

Address _____

City _____*State*_____*Zip*_____

Send to: **Outcomes Unlimited Press, Inc.**   ***Phone orders call:***
1015 Gayley Ave. Ste.#1165   ***(213) 208-2952***
Los Angeles, CA. 90024

BIBLIOGRAPHY

*ADVANCED TECHNIQUES OF HYPNOSIS AND THERAPY:
SELECTED PAPERS OF MILTON H. ERICKSON, M.D.* edited
by Jay Haley
   Grune and Stratton: 1967

*THE BE-HAPPY ATTITUDES: EIGHT POSITIVE
ATTITUDES THAT CAN TRANSFORM YOUR LIFE*
by Robert H. Schuller
   Word Books: 1985

*BOOK OF FIVE RINGS by Miyamoto Musashi
   Bantam Books: 1982*

COMMUNICATION, FAMILY, AND MARRIAGE edited
by Don Jackson
   Science and Behavior Books, Inc.: 1970

COMPREHENSIVE TEXTBOOK OF PSYCHIATRY/IV edited
by Harold I. Kaplan, M.D. and Benjamin J. Sdack, M.D.
   Williams and Wilkins: 1985

THE CREATIVE PROCESS IN THE INDIVIDUAL
by Thomas Troward
   Dodd, Mead, and Company: 1915

THE EDINGURGH LECTURES ON MENTAL SCIENCE by
Thomas Troward
   Dodd, Mead, and Company: 1909

FROGS INTO PRINCES by Richard Bandler and John Grinder
   Real People Press: 1979

*THE GREATEST SALESMAN IN THE WORLD: PART II
by Og Mandino*
   Bantam Books: 1988

KEYING: THE POWER OF POSITIVE FEELINGS

HIGHER CREATIVITY: LIBERATING THE UNCONSCIOUS FOR BREAKTHROUGH INSIGHTS by Willis Harman, PhD. and Howard Rheingold
    Institute of Noetic Sciences Book: 1984

HOLY BIBLE: REVISED STANDARD VERSION
    Thomas Nelson and Sons: revised 1952 from 1611 ed.

HOW TO MAKE YOURSELF MISERABLE by Dan Greenburg
    Random House: 1966

HUNA: THE ANCIENT RELIGION OF POSITIVE THINKING by William R. Glover
    Huna Press: 1979

IDEALS OF THE SAMURAI: WRITINGS OF JAPANESE WARRIORS edited by Gregory N. Lee
    Ohara Publications: 1982

INFLUENCING WITH INTEGRITY by Genie Z. Laaborde
    Science and Behavior Books: 1984

LET THERE BE LIGHT: THE SEVEN KEYS by Rocco A. Errico
    Devorss and Company: 1985

LOVE, MEDICINE AND MIRACLES by Bernie S, Siegel, M.D.
    Harper and Row: 1986

LOVING EACH OTHER: THE CHALLENGE OF HUMAN RELATIONSHIPS by Leo F. Buscaglia, Ph.D.
    Fawcett Columbine Books: 1984

THE MAGIC OF BELIEVING by Claude M. Bristol
    Prentice-Hall, Inc.: 1952

THE MIND BODY EFFECT by Herbert Benson, M.D.
    Simon and Schuster: 1979

PATTERNS OF THE HYPNOTIC TECHNIQUES OF MILTON H. ERICKSON, M.D.II by John Grinder, Judith Delozier and Richard Bandler
    Meta Publications: 1977

PEOPLEMAKING by Virginia Satir
Science and Behavior Books, Inc.: 1972

POWER OF THE PLUS FACTOR by Norman Vincent Peale
Foundation for Christian Living: 1987

THE POWER OF POSITIVE THINKING: NEW CONDENSED EDITION by Norman Vincent Peale and edited by Ric Cox
Foundation for Christian Living: 1987

PRACTICAL LESSONS IN HYPNOTISM
by Wm. Wesley Cook, A.M., M.D.
Wiley Book Company: 1950

PRACTICAL MAGIC: THE CLINICAL APPLICATIONS OF NEURO-LINGUISTIC PROGRAMMING by Stephen R. Lankton
Meta Publications: 1979

PSYCHO-CYBERNETICS by Maxwell Maltz, M.S., F.I.C.S.
Prentice-Hall: 1960

QUESTIONS AND ANSWERS ON THE SCIENCE OF MIND by Ernest Holmes and Alberta Smith
McBride and Company: 1935

REFRAMING: NEURO-LINGUISTIC PROGRAMMING AND THE TRANSFORMATION OF MEANING by Richard Bandler and John Grinder
Real People Press: 1982

RELEASE YOUR BRAKES by James W. Newman
Warner Books: 1977

THE ROAD LESS TRAVELED by M. Scott Peck, M.D.
Touchstone Books: 1078

THE SECRET OF INSTANTANEOUS HEALING
by Harry D. Smith
Parker Publishing Company: 1965

SECRETS OF THE NINJA by Ashida Kim
Citadel Press: 1981

THE SCIENCE OF RELIGION by Paramahansa Yogananda
Self Realization Fellowship: 1987

*SOLUTIONS: PRACTICAL AND EFFECTIVE ANTIDOTES
FOR SEXUAL AND RELATIONSHIP PROBLEMS* by Leslie
Cameron-Bandler
Future Pace, Inc.: 1985

THE STRUCTURE OF MAGIC by Richard Bandler and
John Grinder
Science and Behavior Books:1975

*THERAPEUTIC METAPHORS: HELPING OTHERS
THROUGH THE LOOKING GLASS* by David Gordon
Meta Publications: 1978

*TRANCE-FORMATION: NEUROLINGUISTIC
PROGRAMMING AND THE STRUCTURE OF HYPNOSIS* by
Richard Bandler and John Grinder
Real People Press: 1981

UNLIMITED POWER by Anthony Robbins
Simon and Schuster: 1986

USING YOUR BRAIN — FOR A CHANGE by Richard Bandler
Real People Press: 1985

*THE WAY OF THE PEACEFUL WARRIOR: A BOOK THAT
CHANGES LIVES* by Dan Millmam
H. J. Kramer, Inc.: 1980

*WHY SOME POSITIVE THINKERS GET POWERFUL
RESULTS* by Norman Vincent Peale
Fawcett Crest Books: 1986

AUDIO CASSETTE REFERENCES

"DR. DOSSEY'S PERSONAL POWER PROGRAM: YOUR COMPLETE SELF-PROGRAMMING GUIDE" by Donald E. Dossey, Ph.D.
Outcomes Unlimited Press, Inc., Audio Division

"GOALS: HOW TO SET THEM, HOW TO REACH THEM" by Zig Ziglar
Nightingale-Conant Corporation

"HOW TO BE A NO-LIMIT PERSON" by Dr. Wayne Dyer
Nightingale Conant-Corporation

"THE IACOCCA TAPES: AN AUTOBIOGRAPHY" by Lee Iacocca
Nightingale-Conant Corporation

"LEAD THE FIELD" by Earl Nightingale
Nightingale-Conant Corporation

"THE NEW MASTERS OF GREATNESS" by Tom Peters
Nightingale-Conant Corporation

"PEAK PERFORMANCE" by Charles Garfield
Nightingale-Conant Corporation

"THE POWER OF POSITIVE THINKING" by Norman Vincent Peale
Nightingale-Conant Corporation

"THE PSYCHOLOGY OF WINNING" by Denis Waitley
Nightingale-Conant Corporation

"THINK AND GROW RICH" by Napoleon Hill
Nightingale-Conant Corporation

"THROUGH THE BRIAR PATCH" by Donald E. Dossey, Ph.D.
Outcomes Unlimited Press, Inc., Audio Division

INDEX

ABOUT THE AUTHOR

Donald E. Dossey, Ph.D. was born in the middle of a cotton patch in California's San Joaquin Valley. The child of share croppers, he picked cotton and followed the fruit crops from the time he was six years old.

As an instructor of clinical psychology at Pepperdine University, and a consultant in conceptual psychiatry for the National Institute of Mental Health, he founded and directed the Crisis Counseling Centers of Southern California.

Dr. Dossey is a behavioral scientist, linguist, a founding father of psychoneurolinguistics and a recognized expert in neuro-linguistic programming™. He is an internationally acknowledged authority on the treatment of fears, phobias and addictions. He is the founder, and currently director, of the Phobia Institute of West Los Angeles and the Stress Management Centers of Southern California.

He has trained professionals throughout the world in his provocative and innovative techniques. Dr. Dossey has tested and adopted a revolutionary new program of telephone home-treatment which has proven to be faster in obtaining results than any other form of one-to-one therapy. He has produced audio cassette Seminar at Home treatment programs that have helped thousands worldwide.

Dr. Dossey is a former Science of Mind minister. He has hosted his own radio shows "It's Time To Live" and "The Fear Buster".

Dr. Dossey is a sought after guest on television and radio broadcasts nationally, as well as programs as far away as Australia and England. He has discussed his innovative and controversial approaches, like Keying, on such programs as "The Oprah Winfrey Show", "The Merv Griffin Show", CBS News, ABC New, and the NBC News broadcasts.

Well known for his wit and rapport with audiences, Dr. Dossey lectures and conducts seminars throughout the world.

He is often described as a "Will Rogers with a Ph.D."

NEW HOME SEMINAR CASSETTE PROGRAMS with DR. DONALD DOSSEY

THROUGH THE BRIAR PATCH: In this Home Seminar Program you will learn all of the concrete tools to predictably master Dr. Dossey's "Seven Step Personal Growth Program." Controlling your mind, controlling your feelings and controlling your actions. How to let go of the past and create a future you can chart with ease; and how to wash away any fears, phobias or stress. Six hours. $150.00

PREDICTABLE COMMUNICATION STRATEGIES: A program with NEW communication techniques to better personal relationships, sales and business outcome. Excellent for strengthening relationships. Great for trainers, managers, sales, & counseling practitioners. 4 hours. $95.00

"KEYING" IN SUCCESS: Teaching his world famous Keying technique, Dr. Dossey explains how to eliminate fear and depression, better your health, enrich love and increase financial security. One hour 20 minutes. $15.00

MAKING RESOLUTIONS WORK: After listening to Dr. Dossey being interviewed by radio KBIG's Phil Reed, making New Year's Resolutions work will be easy and fun. 30 Minutes. $10.00.

BOOKS

KEYING: THE POWER OF POSITIVE FEELINGS: Overcoming Fears, Phobias and Stress $14.95

HOLIDAY FOLKLORE, PHOBIAS and FUN: Mythical Origins, Scientific Treatments and Superstitious "Cures" $14.95

— — — — — — — — — ORDER FORM — — — — — — — — —

(Please add $3.75 for shipping and handling for book and $5.00 for shipping and handling audio cassette programs. Californias add 8 3/4% sales tax.)

❑ Payment enclosed   Please charge my   ❑ Visa ❑ MasterCard

Acct. # _____ Exp. Date_____

Signature_____

Please send me_____

Total Amount $_____Telephone (   )_____

Name _____

Address _____

City _____ State_____Zip_____

Send to: Outcomes Unlimited Press, Inc.   Phone orders call:
              1015 Gayley Ave. Ste.#1165   (800) 444-2524 Ext. 2
              Los Angeles, CA. 90024